Presented to:

. . . .

By:

. . . .

ART and SOUL

AN ARTIST'S REFLECTIONS

LEIGH FITZ

This book is dedicated to:

my husband, JD—
my greatest love
and
dearest friend,

my kids—Anne, Kate, and Michael,
whom I love voraciously,

and my amazing grandkids—
Hayden, Jake, Clara, Hudson, and Emma,
for whom this book was written.

Table of Contents

Introduction   1

Summers

1   My Story ……………………… 5
2   Be Still ……………………… 8
3   Tricks My Dog Taught Me ………… 10
4   Reflect on What I See …………… 13
5   Whom Are You Following? ………… 16
6   The Boy with the Boat …………… 19
7   Places We've Traveled …………… 22
8   The Taste and Touch of Grace ……… 25
9   Morning Prayers ………………… 27
10   A Word I Should Never Say ………… 30
11   Hanging out at Salmon Beach ……… 33
12   Beautifully Paired ……………… 36

Autumns

13   A Defining Moment ……………… 40
14   Clothes that Never Go Out Of Style… 44
15   Nature's Lament ………………… 48
16   The House that Holds My Home …… 50
17   Peace Like a River ……………… 54
18   Holy Spirit Fruit ………………… 56
19   Longings ………………………… 59
20   Shine on Me ……………………… 61
21   No Doubt About It ……………… 64
22   Chaotic Beauty ………………… 68
23   God's Tender Love ……………… 70
24   Words Aptly Spoken ……………… 74

Winters

25   Am I Ready for Christmas? ………… 76
26   Even the Wind and Waves Obey Him … 78
27   Don't Miss the Memory …………… 82
28   Safe Within ……………………… 84
29   Generosity……………………… 88
30   Finding Warmth in Winter ………… 90
31   List Making ……………………… 94
32   Weeping with God ……………… 96
33   A Glimpse of Heaven …………… 98
34   Colors of My Palette …………… 102
35   Gifts Given in the Dark ………… 105
36   Winter's End …………………… 108

Springs

37   The Wake-up Call ……………… 114
38   The Seed of Discontent ………… 120
39   Hope Ahead …………………… 122
40   Meet Me Half Way ……………… 125
41   Looking for Joy ………………… 128
42   Wake up and Live Your Dreams …… 131
43   Beginnings in Brooklyn ………… 134
44   Help When Helpless …………… 139
45   Mother's Day …………………… 142
46   Before the Cock Crows ………… 146
47   Age before Beauty ……………… 148
48   Afterglow……………………… 152

Abundant Thanks   155
About the Author   157

"Every person is the painter of his own life; choice is the craftsman of the work,
and the virtues are the paint producing the image."
— Gregory of Nyssa

Introduction

Within the pages of this book you will see glimpses of my soul through my art and writings. My story speaks of my musings, my discoveries, my beliefs, my dreams, and my nightmares of loss and woundedness. These are words and brushstrokes that haven't always come easily as I've reflected on the "deeper things of life," through the seasons of my life. With this in mind, the writings and paintings are presented in seasonal sections, although they may not always fit neatly into those categories, as the thoughts and feelings are timeless.

At times, doubt looms over me, obstructing my way forward. When there are no words that adequately reflect the thoughts of my soul, I paint—and through the process of creating, I find my voice. When my brushstrokes fail to render a resemblance of my emotions, I write—filling in the spaces, enhancing the interpretation of the painting. My artwork intertwines with the reflections of my heart, bringing both art and soul to my narrative. My hope is that you feel invited into my story and inspired to pen or illustrate your own.

God, may the words that I write
and the brushstrokes I create
be acceptable in Your sight,
and bring a smile to Your face.
I lay them down before You,
as my offering of gratefulness,
knowing, full well,
I can do nothing apart from You.
~Leigh

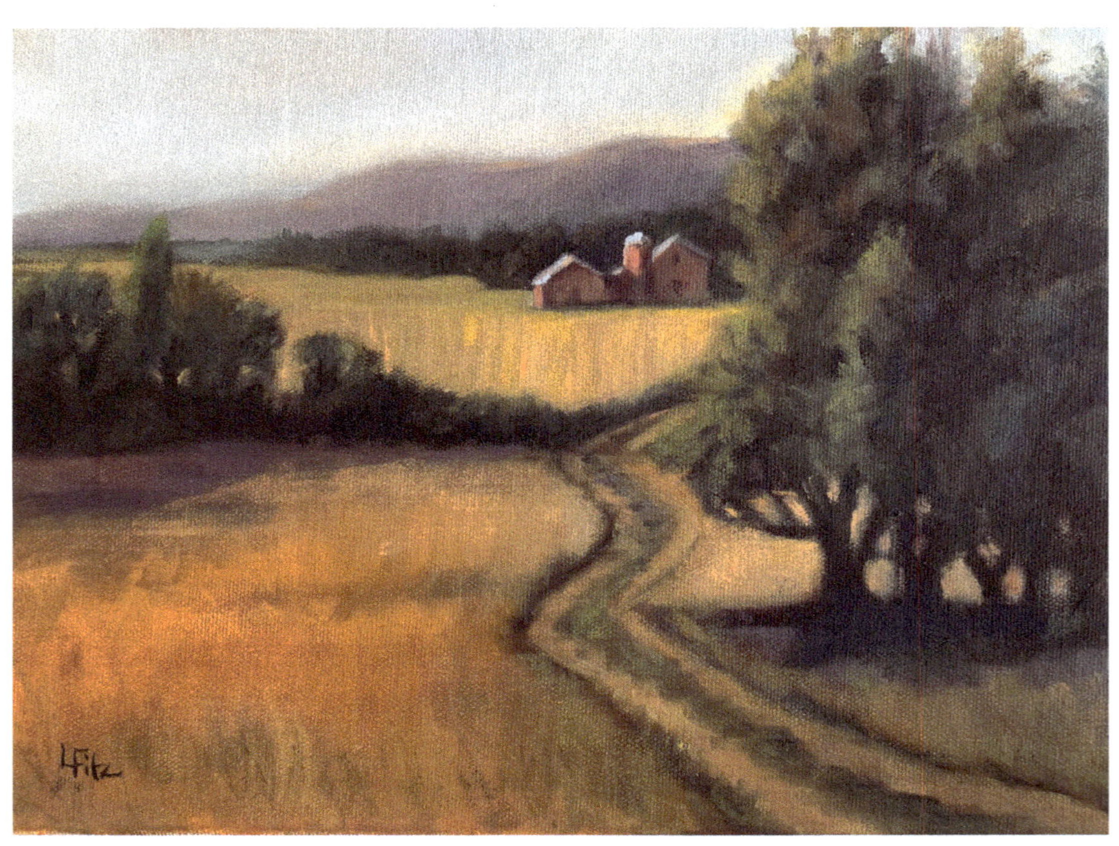

OIL PAINTING, *COMING HOME,* ©2021 LEIGH D. FITZ

Summers

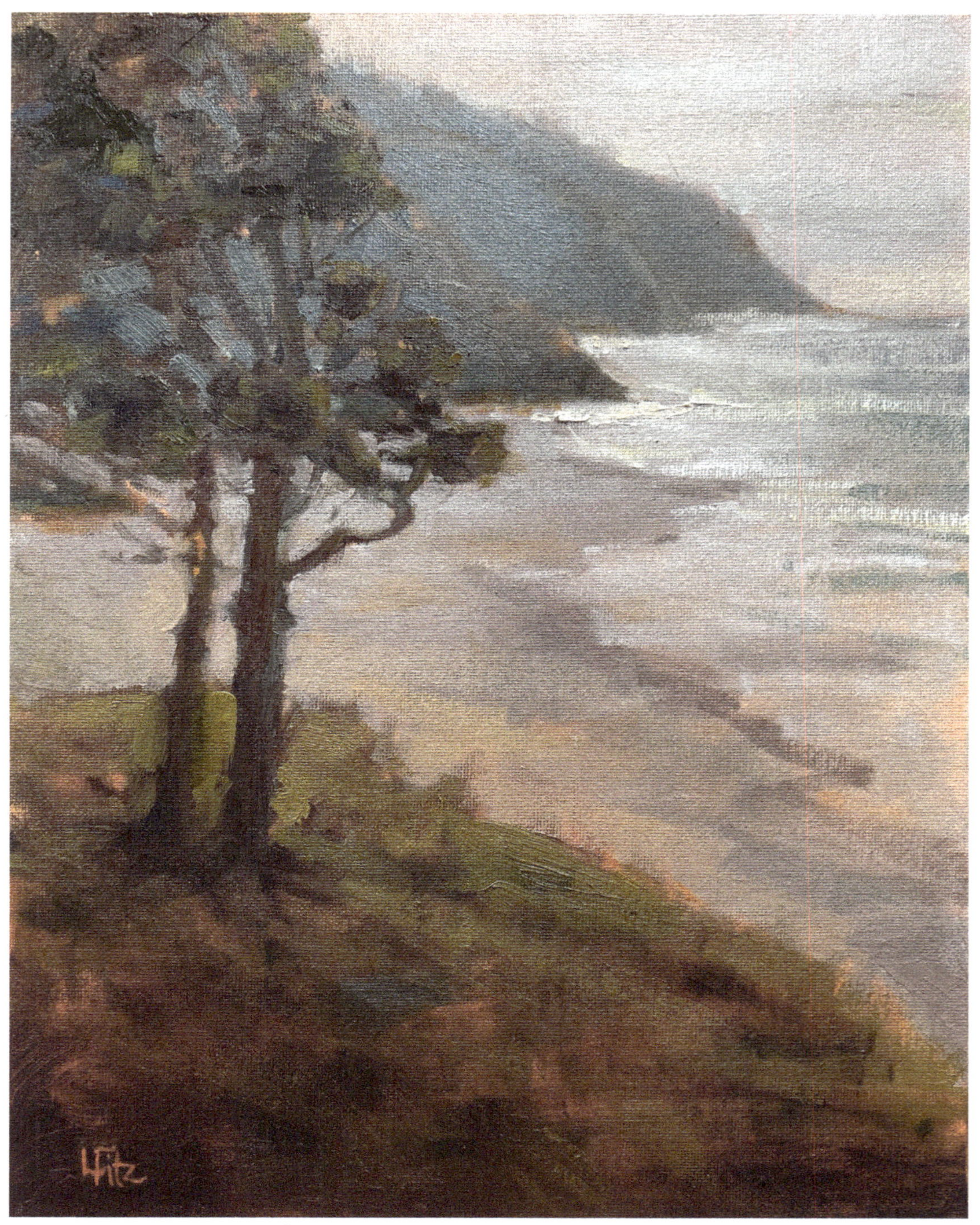

OIL PAINTING, *CALMNESS ON THE COAST,* ©2019 LEIGH D. FITZ; WRITING, 2008

My Story

I held tightly to the word "calmness" as I painted while standing on the Oregon Coast. I was taking a "plein air" workshop, which is a French term meaning "in the open air." One of the instructors encouraged us to choose an emotion or word that each of us wanted to convey in the painting. I attempted to portray calmness on canvas, while taking deep breaths to calm my spirit, desiring to be free of any anxiety or the pressure to perform.

I haven't gone back to touch up this painting, nor do I want to. Like many days in the book of my life, it's not perfect, nor does it feel finished; it is merely an impression of that one day. I will bring the learnings I gathered and take them with me, incorporating them into my future work.

This happens in life, too, although I don't completely understand how our "minds," our "hearts," or our "souls" collaborate to form a person. I can't comprehend the infinite ways nature and nurture come together to create an individual. I can only speak for me.

This isn't a book of persuasion or the touting of my beliefs, writings, or artwork, but rather my responses, impressions, and reflections on my journey of life. I share about the crutches that have aided me as I've limped along, the Light that has illuminated my paint strokes, the people who have spoken compassion and wisdom into my spirit, and the God who I believe witnessed and accompanied me every step of the way. This is my story, but my hope is that you'll see bits and pieces of your story, as well.

My own life changes like the weather and sometimes gets out of control before I even realize I've strayed far from who I am or whom I long to become. When that occurs, I understand that I've lost my story. I often allow circumstances and/or others to control my self-worth, leading me to the conclusion I'm not good enough, smart enough, pretty enough, and . . . certainly not worthy enough to be loved.

I don't want my story to be about trials, loss, rejection, pain, or doubt, but the reality is all these things seemingly show up from nowhere, intent on destroying my confidence. I can't control the troubles of the future or even the present, but I can arm myself and decide how I will react or let them shape me. I have to decide whether to give something or someone the power to murder my dreams or yank me from my focus, luring me down a road full of negativity.

Sometimes, I have to begin again, rereading the last couple of chapters, to prompt me before I get into the rhythm of my narrative. Because I'm a visual learner, painting has aided me in the assimilation of thought and memory. I have to decide how I want to live within my story each day. I resonate with these words I once read, "This is my only life. And it is a great and terrible and short and endless thing, and none of us come out alive."

How do you want your story to end? What's going to be the takeaway for others who read your life? Does it matter?

It matters to me, so I find it helpful to push aside doubt and think forward a bit to imagine what I want my week to look like—or my year, and often my entire life. But I don't live alone; I have a husband. I have adult children, adorable grandchildren, and I want their stories to be interwoven with mine, to add strength to my narrative. I strive to listen to their stories while still being true to who I am. It's a delicate balance. I ponder their lives and the individuals they are becoming. Because of my great love for them, I desire each one to be a prominent character in my journey—to have chapters about their lives and how they profoundly touched mine.

Have you ever wished you could have a "do over"? I have craved the chance to start all over again in hopes of "doing" it better. But I'm coming to appreciate the words of C.S. Lewis, "You can't go back and change the beginning, but you can start where you are and change the ending."

Did your story go on without you, and you're no longer the main character? Are you living out somebody else's dream? I invite you back into your own. I will pass along to you some advice that has stuck with me since I first read it—a phrase that prompted these musings: "Pick up your pen. This is your story now."

So far, it's been a good story, my life: heartbreak, restoration, being uprooted and replanted. It has been full of weeping, laughter, redemption, struggle, loss, hope, love, discovery, recovery, acceptance, a marriage, kids, grandkids, close friends, failure, and success. The good news is I'm still here, so my story isn't finished. I want to keep writing new chapters and I want to come up with a good ending.

According to Donald Miller, author of the book *A Million Miles in a Thousand Years,* a great story is about a hero who overcomes an obstacle to get to a goal. So, what to do when you are in your sixties and tired of having hurdles to jump over? Jumping hurts my bones! I'm slowing down, doing less, caring less about things and hopefully more about people, but somehow that doesn't provide a "page-turner" ending. So now what? Should I increase my time spent painting, write more, and create time to be more involved with family and friends or volunteer for a cause? Relying on or retelling what I've done or accomplished in the past doesn't necessarily make good content for the next chapter or future episodes.

At age eighty-five, when asked what his greatest achievement was, Henry Ford simply responded, "The next one." Maybe age doesn't matter. What I value is to continue to keep living a life worthy of the God I believe in, loving people well, and encouraging others in their pursuits and dreams. I never want to stop leaning fully into each day. I don't want to sit in the bleachers watching someone else, or give up on what or how God may want to employ me in the future. In other words, there's no retirement when you're writing your story. You keep living out your life, page by page, chapter by chapter, until there isn't any more time or space left for words — and the final period stands alone.

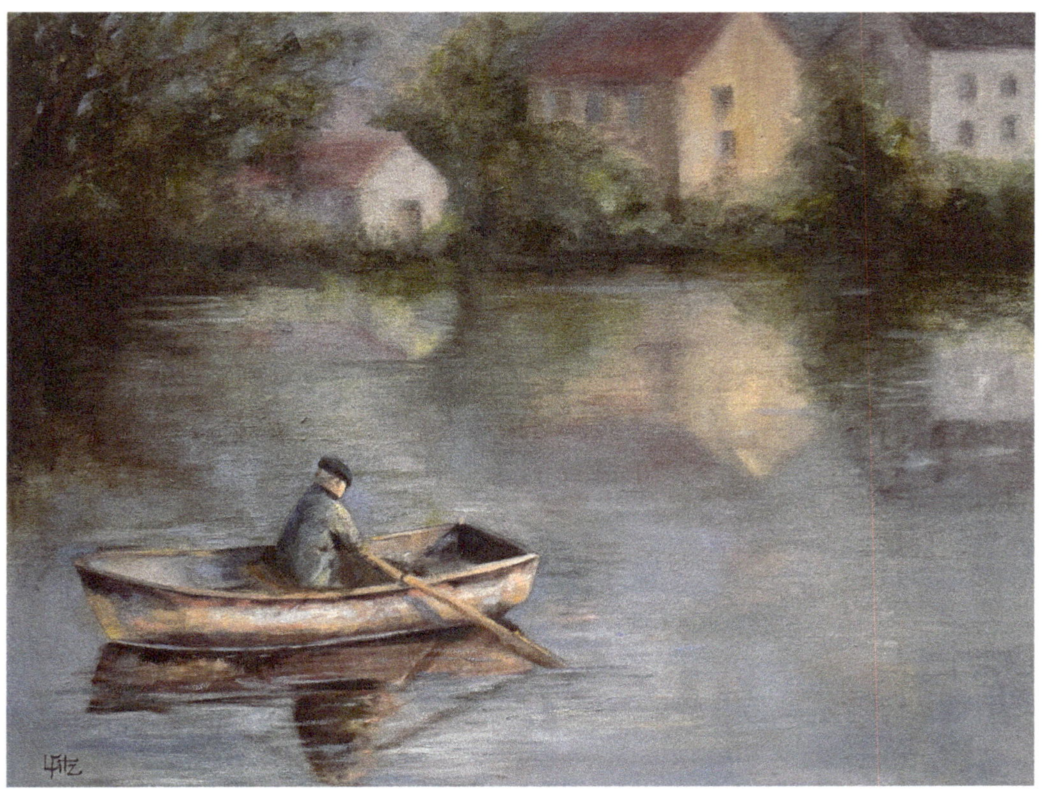

OIL PAINTING, *STILLNESS,* ©2005 LEIGH D. FITZ

Be Still

Several years ago, while visiting Prague with my husband, JD, I noticed a gentleman out in the middle of the "lazy" river, sitting very still in an old boat. There were no signs of a fishing pole in sight, no cell phone, no one else with him. I imagined him peacefully sitting in stillness as he waited for the sun to rise. Once I returned home and began painting this image on canvas, the verse, "Be still and know that I am God,"[1] kept cycling through my thoughts. I wanted to capture the essence of stillness with my brush strokes.

"Being still" in our fast-paced and demanding world is certainly not an easy—or a highly valued—practice. Our electronic devices distract us, and we confuse their interruptive busyness with personal fulfillment. Social

1. Psalm 46:10, NIV

media beckons us to respond, our work demands time, and there is constant pressure to "keep up" and not fall behind. Production is revered and being still is sometimes equated with laziness, wasting time, or a luxury for people who have excessive free time.

I have discovered a more peaceful option.

To experience this stillness, with its absence of noise, is a primary reason for me to get out of bed in the morning, hopefully before the sun rises. No one will be calling or texting, there will be no demands from others, no conversations that need to be maintained— just a simple and quiet sense of calm. There is a "letting go" of yesterday's concerns in the hushed silence of a new day. This is a time of "in between," when the night is slowly fading, but the morning hasn't fully arrived with its responsibilities and to-do lists.

The word for "still" in Hebrew means "to slack, cease, stop striving, let alone, stay, just be," but it is derived from another Hebrew word. This word, *rapha*, means: "to mend, to cure, heal as a physician, repair, and thoroughly make whole." I imagine that when I'm still before my Creator, there is a mending that takes place that I'm not even aware I need. This stillness provides preventive health care for my mind, my body, and my soul. I step aside from life in order to be made whole before I step back in.

In this sacred space of quiet, I ask God to settle my emotions, keep my worries at bay, and give me ears to listen to His gentle whispers. I ask Him to bring to mind any mistakes that need to be made right. I believe a supernatural "stirring" occurs as my heart is softened towards others. This transformation seeps into me as I take a second look at yesterday's reactions—the situations in which I was critical, hurried, or harsh. In stillness with God, there is a "healing" of my spirit.

At these times of quiet, I'm reawakened to the fact that God is present, covering me with a blanket of peace that stills my soul to its core, even in the midst of many cares and concerns. He is a mender of my fear.

It's an extraordinary thought that God and I can sit alone. Other times I think, *How could I have the audacity to presume that the God of the universe, the Omnipresent One, chooses to be alone with me, listening to my thoughts as we confide in each other?* I feel as though He breathes into me an inner calm. He longs for me to trust in Him as He escorts me back into a life filled with relationships, tasks, general busyness, and even the mundane details.

I consider one of my life's greatest lessons is the value of creating space for stillness—to invite it in, silence my soul, and turn down the world. Over the years, I have developed a desperation for this peaceful time of "in between." It's no longer a discipline but a "get to." Even when I'm slammed with stress and when the pressures of life weigh me down, God beckons me to a quiet place of peace. I believe He is offering it to all of us. We need only to take the time to silence our cell phones and be still.

At my age, managing a boat on my own might be a bit tricky, but my comfy recliner sure works well.

"Be still and know that I am God."

(Psalm 46:10, NIV)

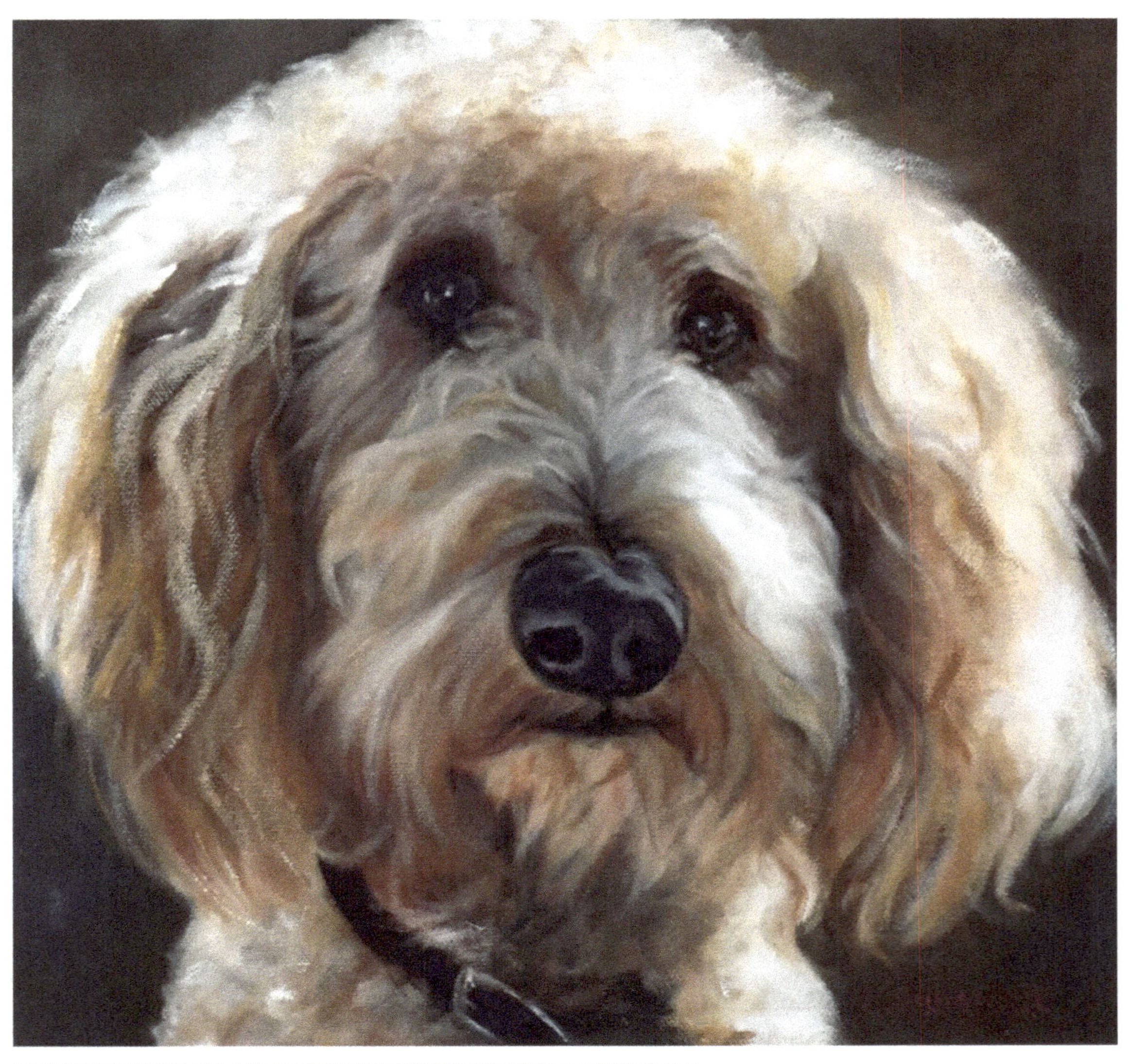

OIL PAINTING, *TUCKER*, BY MY DEAR FRIEND AND ARTIST LINDA HUMMEL; WRITING, 2016

Tricks My Dog Taught Me

Determined that my puppy, Tucker, would be the best-trained dog ever, I taught him all kinds of tricks, such as to sit, stay, high five, speak, whisper, and play hide and seek with toys. Getting him to "come" was the hardest, especially when he was off-leash and outside. He would much rather chase the neighborhood cats than obey me—hard to imagine, I know! I have been frustrated by his inconsistent obedience, but he has also captured my heart and I adore him. To be quite honest, though, he has taught me a thing or two, as well.

Originally, I had hoped Tucker would be a service dog for me as my hearing declined. I no longer hear my doorbell, but he sure does and I hear his bark. And if my hearing aids are out and I'm in bed, I can't hear my house alarm or the smoke detector, but Tucker hears them and he howls at the sound, alerting me to danger. (I hear his howls, since he sleeps on the floor up against my side of the bed!) It would have been nice if I could have taught him to fetch my keys or put his toys away or dust the furniture, but try as I might, he doesn't do housework.

I've heard a lot of people say that they "rescued" their dog and I commend them for it, but frankly, I think Tucker rescued me. He saved me from isolation and self-absorption, and he gave me a new way to see my behaviors and laugh at myself.

Despite the fact that Tucker doesn't always come when called or clean up after himself, he has taught me to be friendlier, like him, when I pass someone in the street. In fact, he's willing to stop and greet total strangers! And although this takes me out of my comfort zone, I've learned that I, like Tucker, can encourage people when pausing to connect, and I am encouraged in return. Tucker has introduced me to neighbors that I have only ever waved to from afar over the years. Now I have the privilege of calling them friends. Admittedly, I've never licked anyone I just met—he's got that one on me!

Teaching Tucker to behave appropriately has caused me to think about whether I always behave appropriately. I wish Tucker would learn not to bark at my friends. Similarly, I need to speak more kindly to my husband, rather than bark orders. Tucker is much too big to be jumping up on people, but I realize that I shouldn't be "jumping" on people with my judgment. We both have the capability of hurting people and need to understand the implications of our actions.

One of the best tricks I've taught Tucker is to "stay," unleashed, outside of our local Starbucks where I frequently drink coffee and meet some of the friends to whom Tucker has introduced me. He sits for long periods on a raised platform, and doesn't budge until I return. People stop to pet him, he is greeted by other dogs, selfies are often taken, and he's adored by children, but Tucker stays put. He is friendly but he keeps his eyes glued on me through the window. He waits for my command, "Okay," before he will get down.

He didn't learn this behavior overnight. It took days and weeks of consistently teaching him to wait and watch for my command. At first, he would bark when I didn't come back after a few minutes, and I'd have to stick my head out the door and say, "No bark!" and remind him to wait.

I realized as I continued to remind him to sit, stay, and wait, that God may be telling me the same words: *Sit with Me, stay close, wait patiently, I haven't left you.* And, quite frankly, following these commands is not always easy for me, but over time I've learned that trusting and obeying Him is invaluable. God has brought me wisdom, joy, and contentment, even when I "bark" or "jump up." He still adores and instructs me when I run away when called or told to stay. And I'm learning that I can reap the "rewards" or blessings when I am willing to sit, stay, and wait with my God.

It turns out you can teach an "old dog," or an old gal, some new tricks!

"But ask the animals, and they will teach you, or the birds of the air and they will tell you
or speak to the earth and it will teach you which of all these does not know
that the hand of the Lord has done this? In his hand is the life of every creature
in the breath of all mankind."
(Job 12:7, NIV)

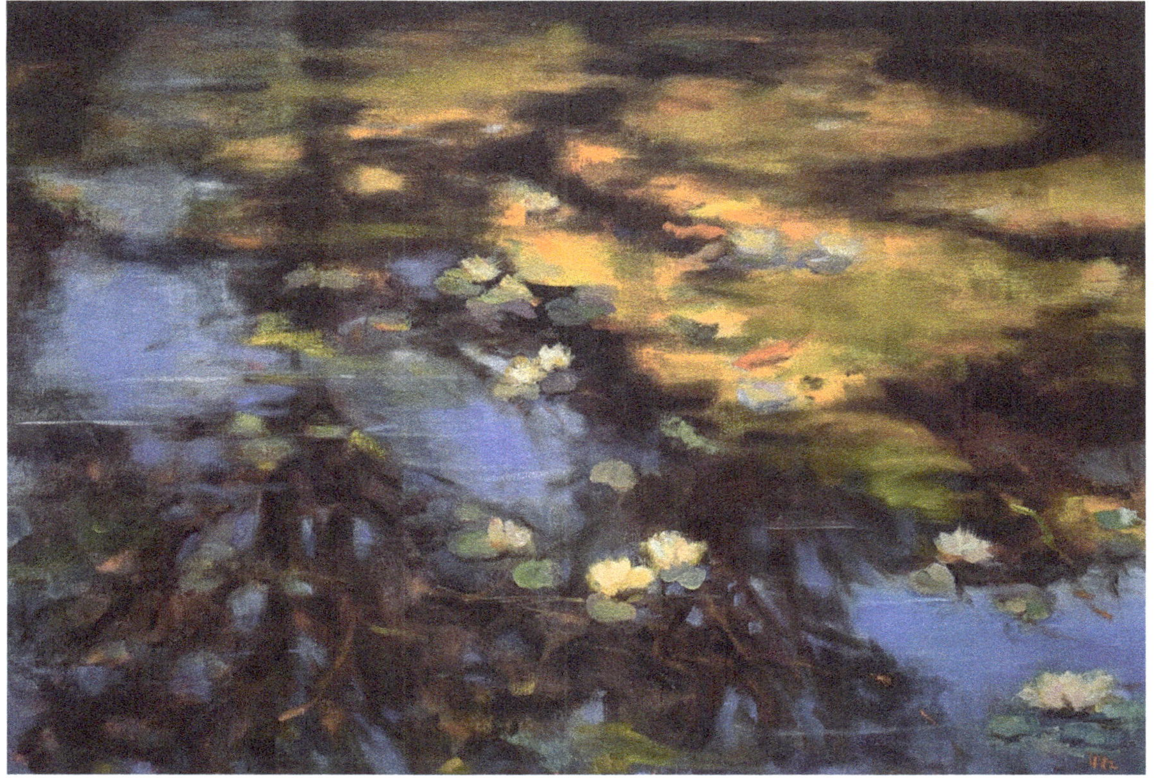

PAINTING, *REFLECTION,* © 2010 LEIGH D. FITZ

Reflect on What I See

I look at this painting and, depending on my mood, often see it quite differently. Some days it feels light and joy-filled, but other days I see the yellow surface of the pond and assume it's algae and wonder what lies at the bottom. I never liked swimming in small lakes or ponds because their unrevealed bottoms seemed dark and mysterious. I didn't trust them, fearing for the safety of my toes. I much prefer the sea with white sand beach beneath me!

Reflect on What I See

I look at myself
And reflect on what I see
No judgment, I just wonder
Am I the person I want to be?

Stepping to the side
I watch myself walk by
What are my actions saying,
Or the expressions in my eyes?

My speech and behavior
Through the lens that others see
What's their interpretation
As they glance and look at me?

What excuses for my actions,
For the toxic muck in my life,
Blurring the person I long to be
Fear? Envy or strife?

Do I respect the way I'm living?
If so, I give applause
If not, I could examine,
Time to reflect and pause.

Then in quiet stillness,
Whispered prayers to guide,
Empowered to live worthy,
I walk on, God by my side.

Socrates said, "An unexamined life is not a life worth living." As I read that line today, it caused me stop and pen this poem and ponder my words and actions over the last few days as my husband and I shelter in place during the COVID-19 pandemic. I'm stepping aside to observe myself, like peering into the still waters of a pond to take a glimpse at my reflection. So far, I haven't been amazed by beauty!

At the time I painted this, years ago, I was focused on the reflection of the brilliantly blue sky and the tall trees waving their beautiful branches to the sun. But gazing at this painting now prompts me to think about what dwells in the depths of this pond, what exists and breathes beneath my surface. *Do I truly know what is dying or decaying on the floor of my soul?*

As I have experienced loss over the years, I have noticed how bitterness can seep down into the core of me, causing my joy to decay and changing gratefulness into a gooey muck of resentment. But focusing on my gains instead of my losses allows me to be buoyant on the water of life and grow healthier. When I choose (and choosing is essential here) to be grateful for all the big and small things in life—joy erupts!

I have read that too much muck or silt (the decay of organic matter that smells like rotten eggs) at the pond's floor can reduce water quality and clarity, creating a toxic environment for fish or other organisms. But the muck can be removed. By physically dredging the pond and adding oxygen to the water, its health can be restored.

Over time, the "muck" in my life can build up as well and—without proper "dredging"—can lead to a toxic life. The only way I know to remove the "muck" is to ask for God's help. He is my oxygen, and when He treats my condition, all the dead things in the depths of my soul can be "dredged" away, restoring life. The "muck" of guilt, shame, bitterness, discontentment, grumbling, and complaining can cause so much "deadness" to my spirit and prohibit the sun from reflecting the beauty of the sky or letting lily pads bloom. Sometimes my vision is muddied, with not enough clarity to see the joy shining through to my life.

I'm learning to *step to the side to watch myself walk by,* and notice (not judge) what my reflection reveals to me. Then I pause for a little needed tender dredging by God.

———

*"Get rid of all bitterness, rage and anger, brawling and slander,
along with every form of malice. Be kind and compassionate to one another,
forgiving each other just as Christ forgave you."*
(Ephesians 4:31, NIV)

"He leads me beside still waters, he restores my soul."
(Psalm 23:2-3, NKJV)

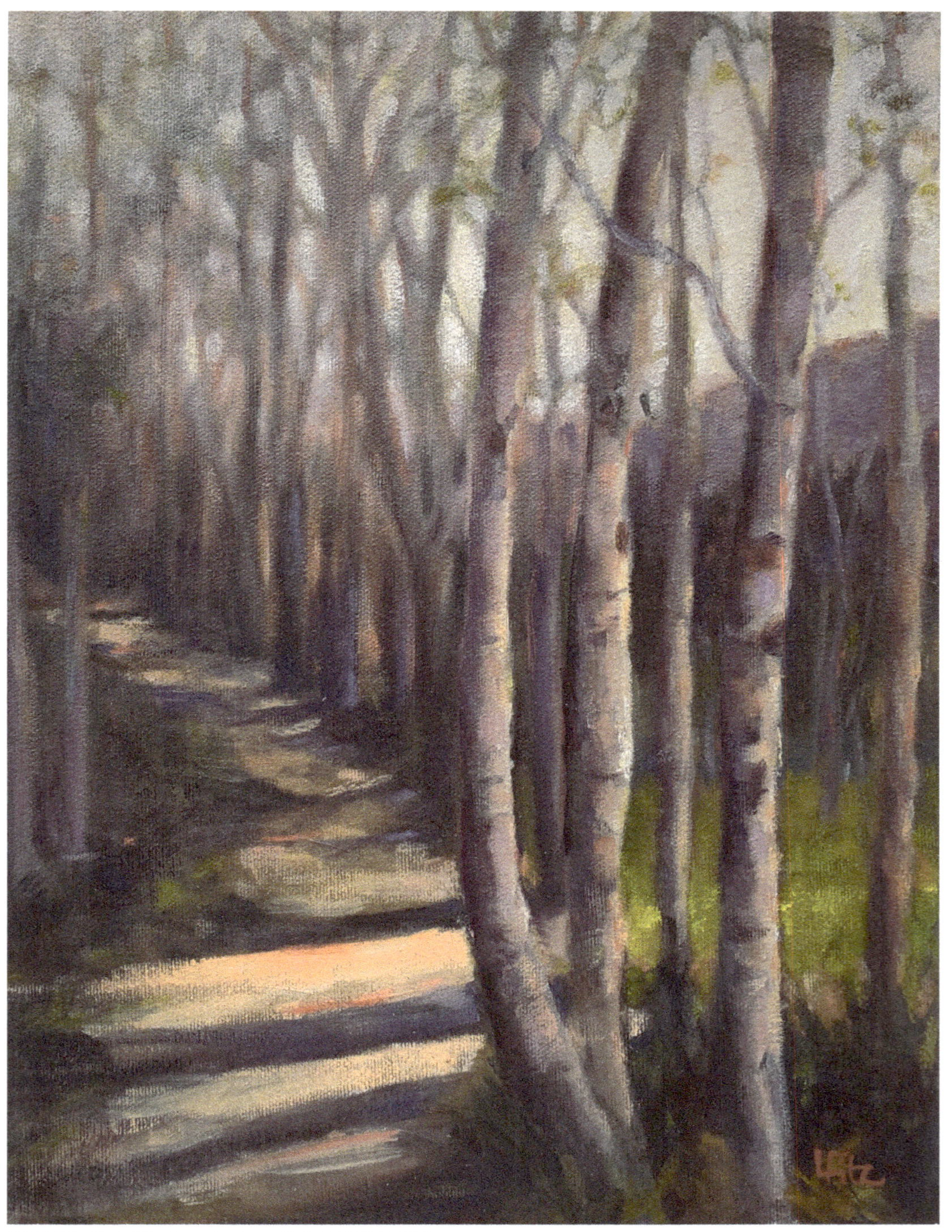
OIL PAINTING, *DOWN UNFAMILIAR PATHS,* © 2019 LEIGH D. FITZ

Whom Are You Following?

"Follow me." That's what Jesus said to His disciple, Peter, and I imagine He is still saying it to us today. Following isn't something we, in our American culture, often like to do. Most of the time we'd rather lead. But there are many benefits to following, and it's not possible for everyone to lead at once.

Following gives us the privilege of observing and experiencing rather than focusing on directions and details. If you are on a hiking trip and have a great trail guide, one who has been there before and knows the way, there is no worry of losing yours. Following your guide grants you the freedom to explore the beauty that surrounds you.

Okay, okay—we all know that life isn't a walk through a forest; it's messier than that. Life has us navigating through throngs of people that are either going the opposite direction or fighting to get ahead of us. Life is a balancing act of responsibilities: family, work, friendships, children to care for, meals to prepare, things to clean, schedules to keep, appointments to arrange, emails to return, and a barrage of text messages that interrupt all of the above so that you lose your train of thought. And never mind doing all of this while you are sleep-deprived and your head is throbbing. All we can do is address the myriad tasks set before us, one step at time.

You tell us to follow You; well, I'm saying, "I don't think so!" I don't have time even to look up! Maybe what's needed is familiarity with the one you are trying to follow. What is he wearing? Does he have an unusual gait as he walks? Do you know whether he ever stops to look back and make sure you are caught up? Does he ask if he can help you with some of those bags of groceries you are carrying or the baby on your hip? Yes, following is either difficult or easy, depending on the character of the one you are following.

This is where trust comes in. I have to be able to trust someone I've committed to follow. Proverbs 3:5-6 tells us, "Trust in the Lord with all your heart and lean not on your own understanding, in all your ways acknowledge him and He will direct your path."

I notice it doesn't say trust in the Lord with all your *mind*. If I analyze God with my head, I lean on my own thoughts, but when I trust Him with my heart, I lean on Him. So I choose to trust in Him with my heart because, deep inside myself I know that I know He is the one and only support system I can lean against without falling.

People will fail me, but God never does. He directs with a great deal more wisdom and love than any person is capable of, because He has my best interest at heart.

But Jesus didn't only say, "Follow Me." He also said (and continues to say), "Cast your cares on Me for I care for you."[2] He says, "Come to Me, you who are burdened and heavy laden and I will give you rest."[3] He says He adores us and has us engraved in the palm of His hand.[4] He says He'll lead us beside still waters and restore our souls.[5] He says He'll never leave us on our own.[6] Now, that sounds like someone I want to follow, someone I can trust to love me enough to guide me through life.

Oh Lord, I will follow You today and see where You lead me, but tomorrow I'm booked solid!

—

"I will lead the blind by ways they have not known,
along unfamiliar paths I will guide them;
I will turn the darkness into light before them and
make the rough places smooth.
These are the things I will do;
I will not forsake them."
(Isaiah 42:16, NIV)

2. 1 Peter 5:7, NIV
3. Matthew 11:28, NIV
4. Isaiah 49:16, NIV
5. Psalm 23: 2b, 3, NIV
6. Deuteronomy 31:8, NIV

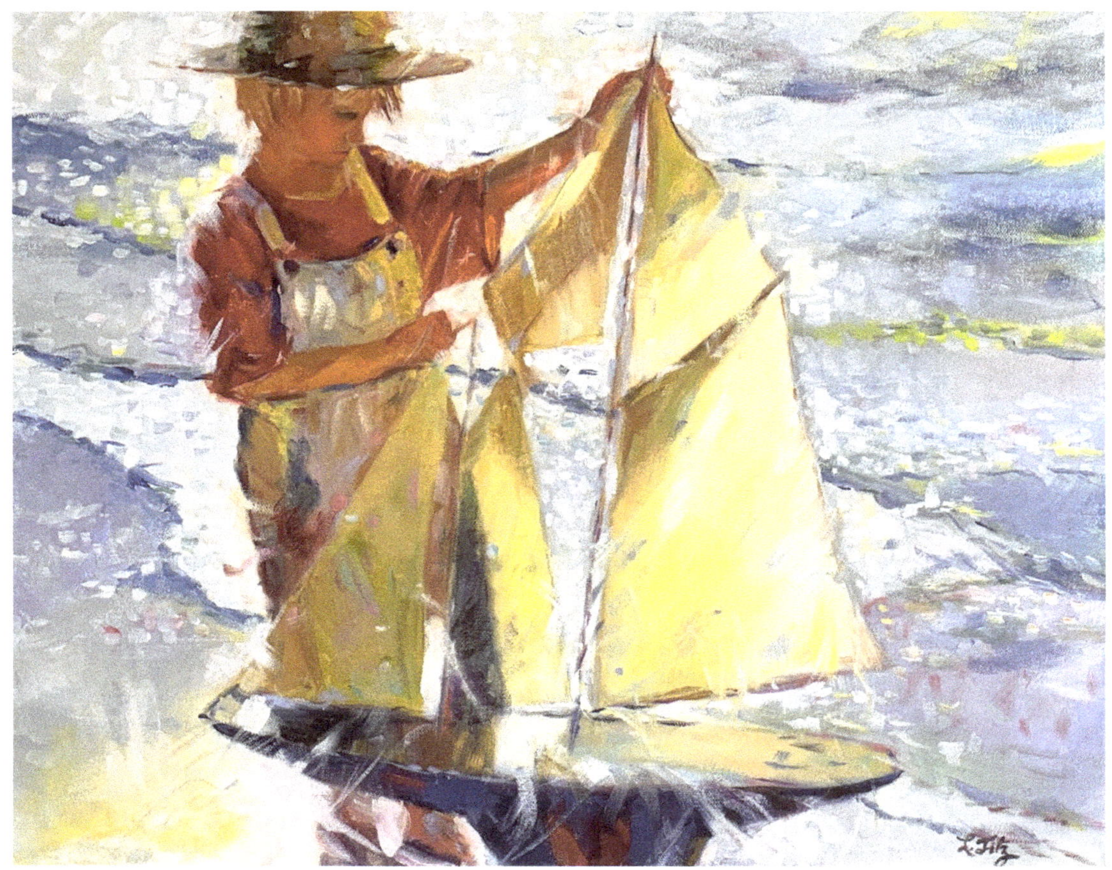

OIL PAINTING, *BOY WITH THE BOAT* © 2007 LEIGH D. FITZ; WRITING, 2017

The Boy with the Boat

This painting always brings a smile to my face. For one, it summons up thoughts of my son as a boy, memories of him playing contently in his overalls, lost in his world of make believe. It also conjures up my favorite memories of my own childhood on the north shore of Long Island.

I imagine, once again, the smells of the sea, seaweed baking in the sun, and the creosote pilings that supported a walkway out to the dock. I remember the laughter, the Good Humor truck that came twice a day with ice cream bars and Dixie cups, the sounds of the waves, seagulls, and wind, and the prehistoric horseshoe crabs that frightened me.

On the beach, I scooped up anything and everything my parents would permit me to bring home: shells, rocks, sea glass, pebbles, lost treasures. I was allowed to venture off down the beach (which, looking back now, probably wasn't far at all). I made up stories of pirates and lost children and inserted myself into these imagined tales; the pirates would kidnap me and then I would make a clever and daring escape!

But, sadly, though I am the one who put the paint on the canvas, I cannot claim the original idea of this painting; I merely copied the original as a way to teach myself to emulate this artist's loose impressionistic style. I only wish I had made a note of the artist's name to give him/her credit for the idea.

The process of copying other artists' work is a way to further my own learning. What drew me to this painting was the use of color and broad strokes. When I visited the Louvre years ago, I watched other artists painstakingly copy a famous painting that hung in front of them. My painting teacher encouraged our class to do this to discover the artist's palette or brushstrokes and gain new insight and skills, so that we might be able to understand how to paint effectively in our own work.

It's a good life lesson, in general, to learn by watching and then attempt to replicate what you see. After tasting a friend's cooking, you may ask for a recipe, so you can attempt to make it as well. You learn from doing. You watch and try to mimic an athlete. You read and collect thoughts from other writers, which in turn influences your grasp of a particular subject and your skill at writing. What's essential in the process is not taking credit for something you didn't create yourself. You may fool everyone, but living with lies is a weighty burden that even the glory of praise can't erase.

I remember as a young teen, copying an abstract portrait of a woman. When I received a compliment, I didn't reveal the truth but took the praise instead. It felt good only for a second, and then guilt and loathing set in faster than you could imagine.

Copying can be a way to explore your passions. Try one on like a piece of clothing to see if it fits. Is it uncomfortable? Do you like yourself wearing it? If not, take it off and try something else. You learn to master that passion in part by learning from others. You can copy other people whom you want to emulate, but ultimately everyone has to determine who we are by ourselves, giving credit along the way to those who have contributed to our learning and success.

I could've spent my life copying other people's paintings, but I had to figure out what brought the most pleasure in creating art for myself. The realization of how much joy it brings me to create emotion, a reflection, meditation, or memories on canvas came to me slowly over the years, but now it plays a vital role in each painting I attempt. My desire as I paint is to stir the emotions and connect to my soul. As I try to solve a myriad of problems with my paintbrush, I also engage my mind to grasp what the painting is teaching me about myself, my God, or everyday life. Painting on canvas has become a hidden counselor that whispers wisdom for my mind, which I hope takes root in my heart and actions.

Comparing my work with others can get me into a heap of trouble, especially when I look at the old masters' paintings. I don't always see the value in my work, but what I do see is that art enables me to learn about life and listen more closely to what I think God is teaching me in the process. I do feel His pleasure when I create. We are kindred spirits in that respect. I marvel at His creativity, doling out compliments, telling Him what I think of His work.

I do get a bit jealous of other artists' work when I'm battling with my paintbrush and not rendering on canvas what I see in front of me! I'm learning to ask for help. I am grateful to my painting teachers and classmates for all the help and encouragement I've been given over the years. As humbling as it is, there will always be more gifted painters or writers who are stellar compared to me. The flip side is that I will be better than others in certain areas as well. But when we help each other, and learn from one another instead of competing, there is the hope of rendering something quite extraordinary.

"As iron sharpens iron, so one person shapes another."
(Proverbs 27:17, NIV)

Note: This essay was written with my grandkids in mind, as they explore various ideas, sports, books, art, and ways to communicate with the world. I hope they each discover their own passions and what gives them joy in the doing!

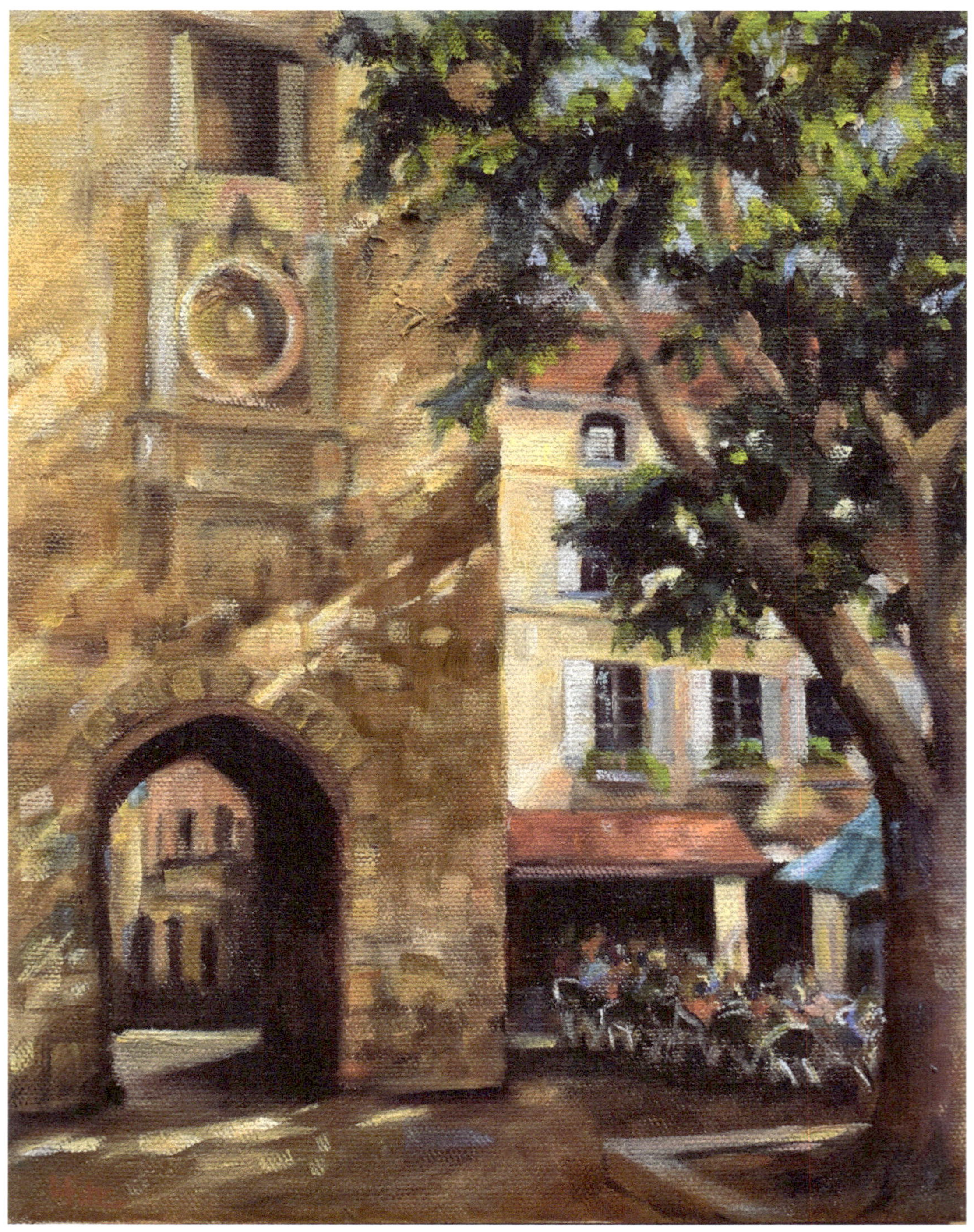

OIL PAINTING, *MAGIC IN THE MOMENTS*, © LEIGH D. FITZ (FRANCE, OUR FORTIETH WEDDING ANNIVERSARY); WRITING, 2019

Places We've Traveled

There's a moment in time, maybe for each of us, when an image jogs our memories and brings a smile to our lips because it represents a time when love grew and happiness reigned. Gazing at this painting takes me back to one of those moments. JD and I were in Aix-en-Provence, France, celebrating our wedding anniversary. My senses are transported in time, coming alive with smell, touch, taste, and sound as they collide with the goodness we found there. It reminds me of a happier place filled with wonderment. I hold tightly to the memory of being within that moment.

To the viewer, this painting is probably just a painting. But to me, it is so much more. What you don't see or feel is the sun continuing to travel down the sides of buildings, filtering through the canopy of trees that gave shade and comfort from the hot afternoon sun. What you don't see is the graceful movement of the leaves being toyed with by the slight breeze and playing with the light. What you don't taste is the crisp, white wine we sipped or the smell of the food we hungrily devoured. What you don't hear is the tingling of glasses, the occasional bursts of laughter, the chatter of the French-speaking people, or the music that spontaneously erupted from young artists that filled the plaza with incredible energy and sound. It's difficult to capture the inner peace that comes after a day well-spent, as you sit with a person you love. Shared moments that last after the sun goes down. A moment you decide to take with you into the future to strengthen your relationship. This was a moment for me when all was right with the world.

Remembering times like this refurbishes my love for my guy today, the importance of which comes when that loving feeling isn't present. I've decided to keep creating moments like this, to keep our love refreshed. This is one of the reasons why, when I return home from a trip, I attempt to paint a small picture of the place we've visited, to remember and represent grace-filled memories we shared. Memories of these cherished times aid us when we encounter difficult ones. Thinking of past, meaningful conversations encourages us to persevere and give grace when current conversations break down into disagreements.

Even as I write these words, I've decided that I'm going to make this day memorable and imagine a fun way to celebrate us. One doesn't have to travel to a distant land to create a magical moment. Maybe it simply takes ordering out for pizza, lighting a candle, and talking about our memories of yesterday's love, creating a moment in the present.

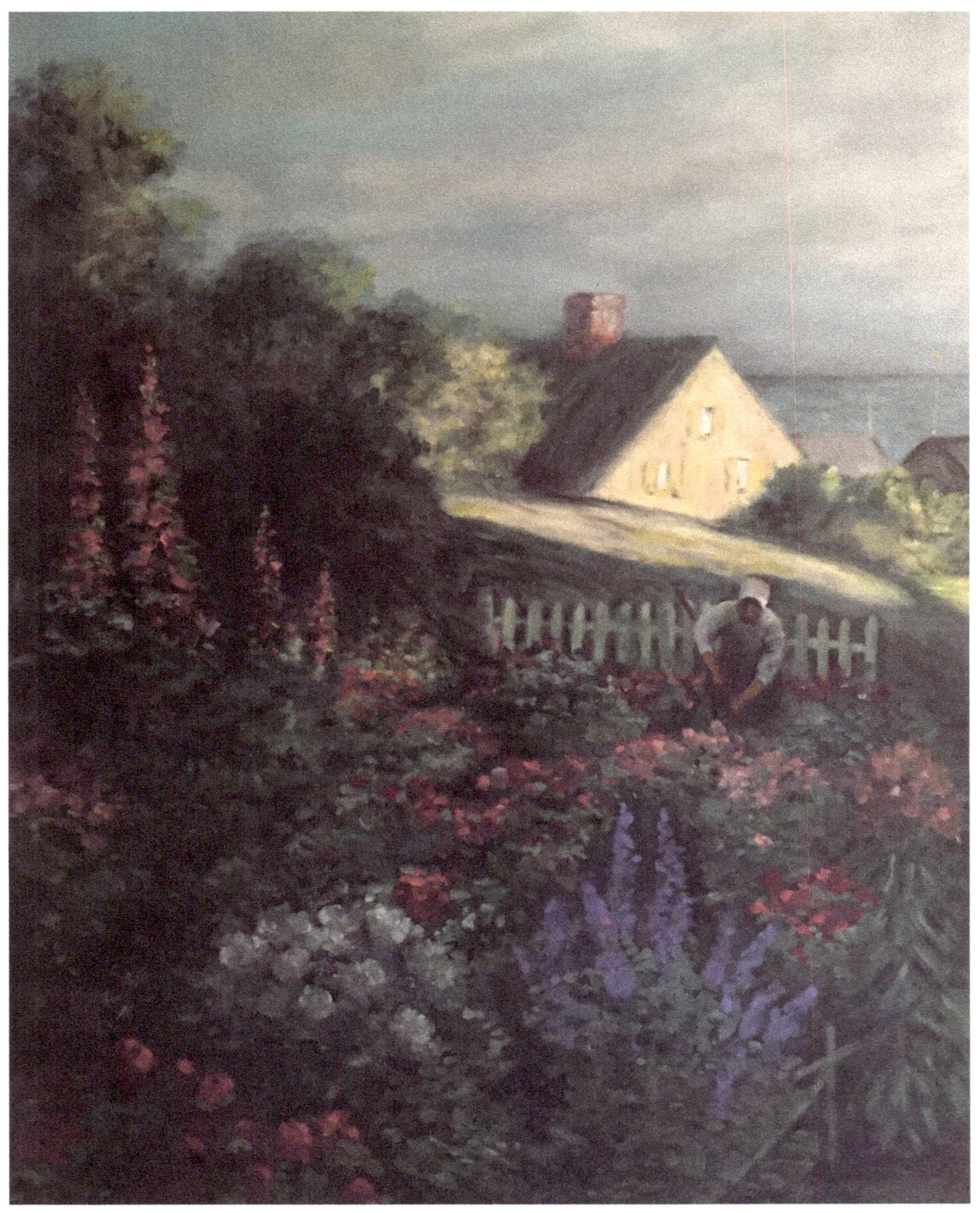

OLD MASTERS PAINTING COPIED FROM A PICTURE IN AN ART MAGAZINE, 2000. ORIGINAL ARTIST UNKNOWN; WRITING, 2019

The Touch and Taste of Grace

I've never fully understood Grace enough to describe it accurately, so I sought to paint a picture to represent it. As I've grown older, I've come to realize it is a word that may indeed be indescribable or unpaintable.

When I first saw Grace I was only a child; it came alongside me and sat close enough that I could smell and touch it. Even as a child, I could sense its presence through people who had Grace within them, like my mom. I didn't know what it was at the time, but I noticed the way it made me feel good inside, like an undeserved hug. I took a nibble of Grace, not knowing what it was made of, and I found it was sweet and savory simultaneously.

Grace kept showing up in songs we sang in church, such as "Amazing Grace," or, "The Wonderful Grace of Jesus." We said "Grace" at the table before meals, and Jesus and Grace always seemed to end up in sentences together. Frankly, the word confused me. Was it a noun, a verb, an adjective? But back then I was too young to ask these questions.

Around the age of five, I said yes to God's Grace before I understood what forgiveness was or what I was saying yes to. My mother told me that I jumped off the pew at church and ran to the pastor in front, who had invited anyone in the audience to come forward to receive Jesus. I didn't know how God would squeeze into my little life, but I liked the idea that He "cleaned" me up inside. Over time, I came to see that the Grace of God meant that I was forgiven for all the wrong I had done, but forgiveness was as intangible a word as Grace.

I had a dad whose presence obscured my sensation of Grace. He was stern and angered easily—even over normal childish behavior. I couldn't make him love me or be proud of me, so I wondered how I could ever meet the expectations of God. Grace seemed to fall away, rather than encompass me as a child. As a result, my relationship with God and His Grace was complicated. My reception of God's intended outreach to me was wrapped in pain.

Although I learned the childhood song that went, "Jesus loves me, this I know, for the Bible tells me so," I wanted to replace the word "Jesus" with "my Dad," and understand the image through an earthly, familial lens. I confused the unconditional, proactive love of God with my father's reactive anger.

Maybe Grace looks and smells differently to everyone. Surely I'm not the only person whose dad, or past, affected her future understanding of wonderful concepts such as Grace and love, in our broken world. I am sensing that my perception of Grace is closely tied to the Grace and forgiveness I offer to others—offering retroactive forgiveness to those who, like my father, blocked my view and vision of God's Grace to me. God's Grace for me continues to come into focus as I give Grace to my father's memory in my early years.

So, what are the colors, sounds, and tastes of this growing clarity and experience of the Grace of God? As I've gone looking for Grace, I have seen it in simple acts of compassion and sacrifice—like when a well-dressed adult, late for work, stops to patiently tie a child's shoe. I feel it from a friend who wraps her arms around me in my sorrow and points out blessings in my journey, even in the presence of unanswered prayers. Grace nestles deep in my soul and covers me, feeling like warm oil being tenderly rubbed into parched skin, relieving the itch. Its flavor is the most exquisite, extravagant meal served lovingly without cost. Its smell is like the fresh scent of laundry drying on a sunlit day. And to me, Grace sounds like loving whispers that calm my fear in the middle of the night when isolation feels imminent.

I painted this image of the Grace of God coming to me in a garden abundant with flowers standing tall, ready to be gathered up and given to others as sweet fragrances and reminders of God's loving Grace to them. I was in my cozy home with a surrounding garden and picket fence. The picture is filled with light, covered by cerulean blue skies and trimmed with pink tinted clouds. To me, it was beautiful beyond belief—unmerited, Grace-filled. The "me" in the painting was fully present and fully recovered (although alone), and living and loving others through God's Grace working in my senses and my creativity.

As I return to my reality from my painting, several life lessons have emerged. The memory of a dear child offering herself to God is Grace. Wrestling with my dad's memory leads me to forgiveness, a reminder of God's Grace to me. Receiving a vision of God with me in my garden, blessing my creativity, is extreme Grace.

So, I return to my "Gratefulness Journal," realizing that Grace is closely tied to thankfulness. When I set my gaze on the horizon and find Grace, I take my eyes off my losses. Grace changes my days. These changed days change my weeks, months, and the trajectory of my years.

Grace abounds. Grace changes me. And, changed, I experience even more Grace.

Grace lives beside you
whether you know it or not.
Grace inhabits your every move
Whether you acknowledge it or not.
Grace keeps getting up close and personal
Whether you move away or not.
Grace brushes your face gently,
causing a smile.
Grace whispers "I love you"
Whether you answer
Or not....

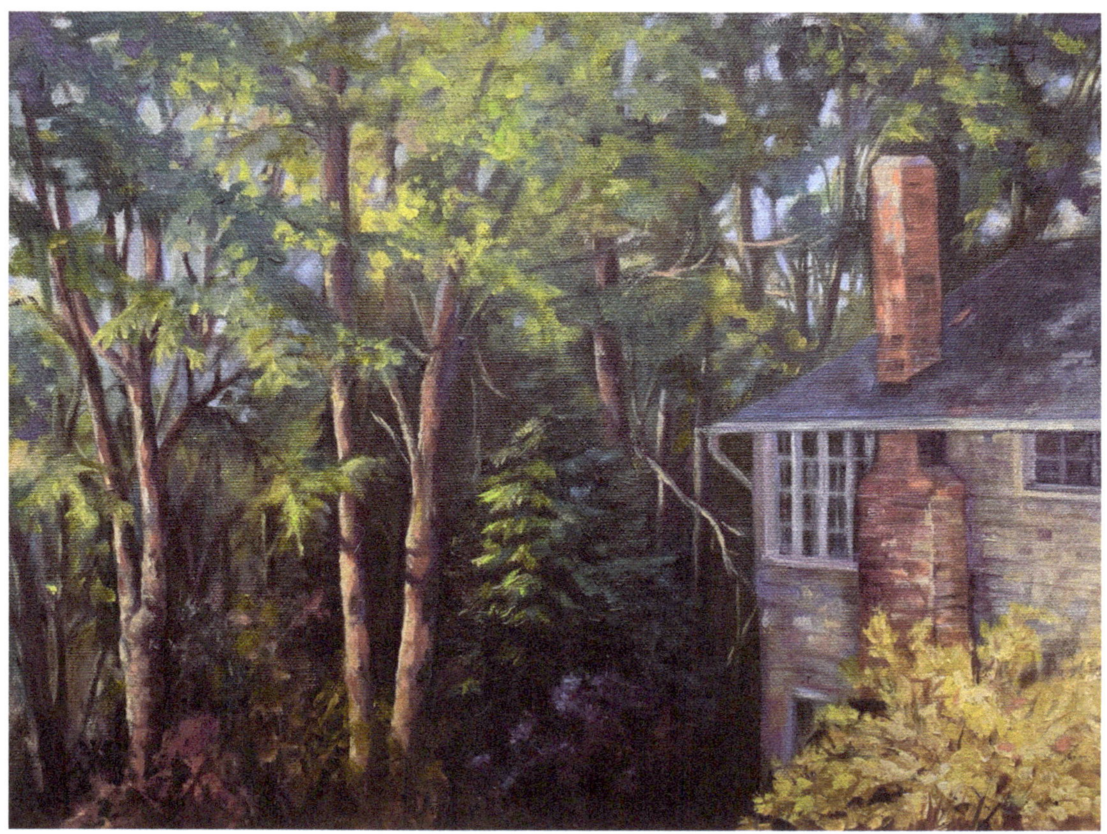

OIL PAINTING, *MORNING PRAYER* © 2007 LEIGH D. FITZ; WRITING, 2018

Morning Prayers

My morning ritual consists of making a pot of tea and some toast, going to a small room upstairs (which long ago was my son's bedroom), kneeling down (though at my age I sometimes skip this to save my knees), and begin my whisperings to God.

As my tinnitus and hearing loss became more severe, so did my depression. Truth be told, I neither wanted to believe I was depressed, nor did I want anyone to tag me with this label. Viewing it wrongly as a weakness or a lack of trust in my God, I didn't explore my options for assistance such as counseling, opening up to a close friend, or taking antidepressants. Consequently, I started spending more time alone. My morning rituals anchored me. My love of reading Scripture and having honest and gut-wrenching conversations with God was my saving grace. Watching the sun rise and transform the trees into sculptures of breathtaking magnificence caused me to ponder whether God would transform me as well. We are all works of God's art.

I've visited my little room each day for over twenty years now. Merely stepping into this sacred space feels as though I'm treading onto holy ground. This is the place I meet God. A place to listen. A place to release my deepest thoughts, a place to weep my confessions, a place to ask questions, a place where I have committed Bible verses to memory and learned from Scripture—and a place I bring and lay before Him names of people, offering up my requests to Him. This is a place where there are pictures of my family, woodcarvings made by my dad, old journals, books and Bibles, a cozy chair, and a view of the forest behind my house. A place of comfort and solitude. A place where I've filled pages of journals with writings that are sometimes hardly readable, with their mis-spelled words and awkward sentences that perhaps only God knows the meaning of. A safe place to be fully exposed—my honest self before Him.

The only problem I come across in this room—the place where my critical eye condemns—is me. I say to myself, *You're not enough, not now, not ever. You're not smart enough, pretty enough, good enough. Why would God want to talk to you? Your life has never amounted to greatness, your name is empty without initials, nobody likes you or really cares what you write or what you think, your artwork is marginal. How can God forgive you when you repeat the same wrongs over and over again? Why would the God of the universe take the time to listen to you? You may think He loves you, but He doesn't.*

I know these condemning comments do not come from God, but sometimes it's hard to convince myself, especially when life gets burdensome and depression has its relentless hold on my life. In this room, I'm learning to leave judgment and condemnation at the door. I imagine the expression on Jesus' face as He enters this space. He's looking at me with love, acceptance, tenderness, and a smile.

This room is where I declare my love for God and He declares His love for me. Some days I come empty and simply say, "I have nothing to give or the energy to receive; can I please just sit in your lap?" He never denies me this request.

This place is where I unload my deepest thoughts, offer my morning prayers, and pen my feelings. God hears all of me in both confession and praise. I just wish my praise was a longer list than my confessions.

Am I high maintenance or what?!

"The Lord your God is in your midst, a mighty one who will save; he will rejoice over you with gladness;

he will quiet you by his love; he will exalt over you with singing."

(Zephaniah 3:17, ESV)

"I rise before the dawn and cry for help."

(Psalm 119:147, NIV)

"Oh Lord, you have searched me and you know me. You know when I sit and when I rise;

you perceive my thoughts from afar. You discern my going out and my lying down;

you are familiar with all my ways. Before a word is on my tongue you know it completely."

(Psalm 139:1-4, NIV)

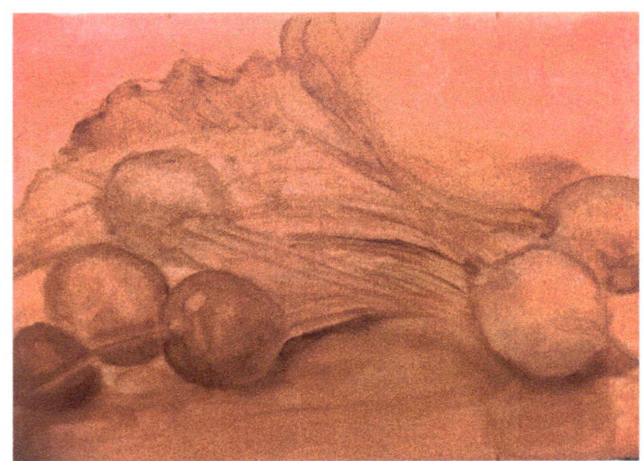 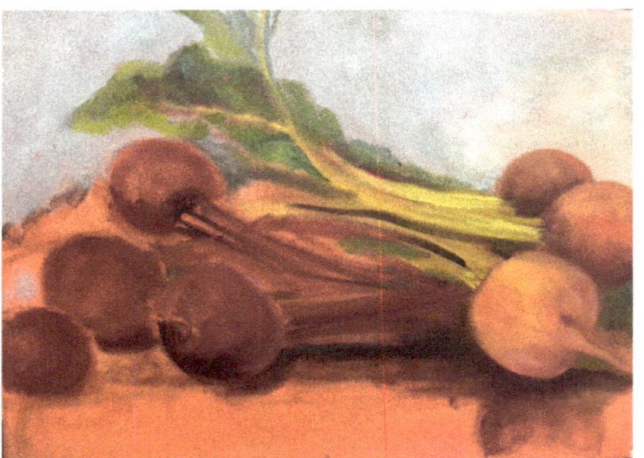

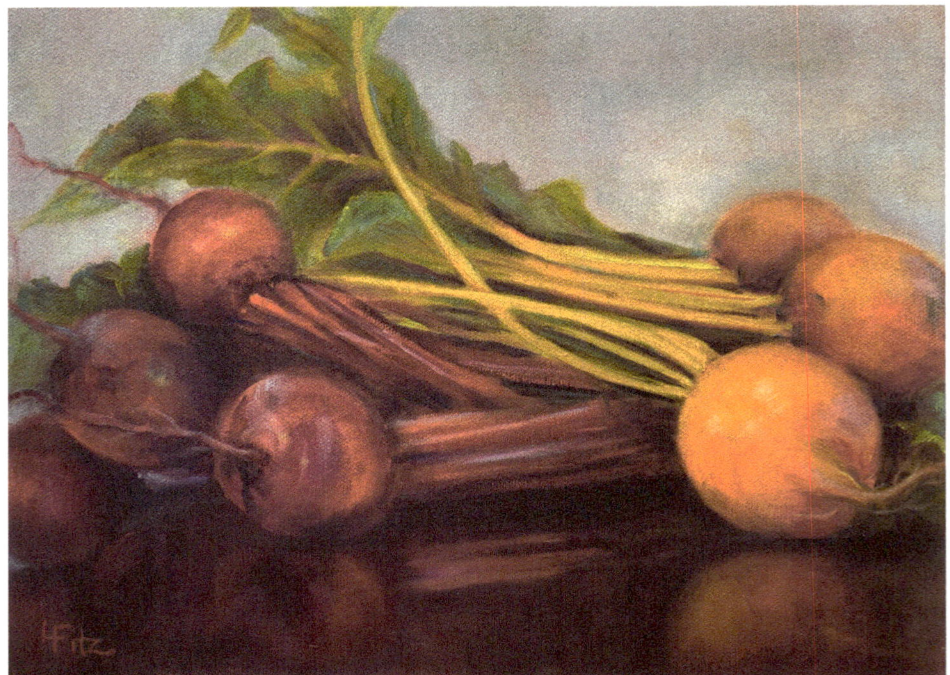

OIL PAINTING, *BEETS ME* © 2018 LEIGH D. FITZ; WRITING, 2020

A Word I Should Never Say

More often than I would like, I "step in it." I do this by carelessly offering unsolicited suggestions or what I perceive to be helpful comments for others to consider—which, much to my chagrin, seem to discourage rather than uplift. I had no idea! What I think is valuable advice or assistance in solving another's problem can be perceived as a form of judgment.

When I volunteer my explanation to those around me, it can come across as a not-so-subtle way of communicating that I think they need my help, or worse, I imply they are not capable. My "encouraging words" can be heard as a message full of *shoulds*, corrections, or judgments, unintentionally indicating the listener needs to change. Unconsciously, maybe, I want them to be a closer version of myself. I have to be careful when I attempt to encourage others; rather than providing suggestions to solve the problem, I should instead be sitting with them in their difficulty, asking questions and listening.

I know I've failed miserably in the past, as I've generously given out heaps of *shoulds* and *oughts*. I even sometimes resort to using Bible verses, intended to offer direction, but those, too, can feel like a subtle form of criticism or judgment when you are on the receiving end. I hide behind the disguise of Scripture—and in the moment I think I'm helping—but in actuality, I am often pouring on guilt instead. So the result of my attempts to encourage is transformed into discouragement. Instead of giving life, I have given a clear message that there is something wrong with their approach and that my way is the "right way." My intentions may be pure, but my tactlessness can leave a person demoralized, disheartened, or resentful.

I'm recognizing we are all on different paths, but sometimes I slip into the thinking that others need to learn the same lessons I'm learning. I assume my truth is suitable for everyone. I often wrongly conclude that the things I'm discovering, others *should* discover as well (again, sorry).

Lessons I'm learning are strictly for my benefit, not for everyone to know. My experiences cannot be others' truth. My journey's path shouldn't be everyone else's trail. What I've gleaned from life perhaps isn't what others need to gather. My truth, sense of beauty, and organization may not be yours.

Writing this book and submitting my writing to my editor can be painful. I see all the markups, corrections, suggestions, and rewrites, and it can be difficult not to take it personally. Discouragement can take over and I'm suddenly back in grade school, with red marks all over my papers, and I feel like a failure. The difference is that I've chosen to hire an editor to correct my grammar and word usage and to offer advice that I can accept, modify, or reject. I expect there will be rewrites that I will have to spend time fixing. I have submitted myself intentionally and need to keep deciding not to take her advice personally. It's a process that will hopefully produce a better book.

But in most of life, we are not each other's editors. People generally don't see their life as a project nor me as their editor. Instead, I think we *should* (there I go again) be each other's sounding board or cheerleader by complementing the good we see. Sometimes people don't want an outside solution. Maybe they want to solve the issue themselves, even if it takes longer or is more difficult. And sometimes people don't want their problem solved at all; maybe they just want to vent or feel heard. As friends, it is important we know how to listen and empathize with each other's struggles, only offering help when asked. Until then, we *ought to* (I can't help myself) listen and be there for each other.

This painting illustrates my point. I started with buying the beets, setting them up and taking pictures, forming a composition, drafting a sketch, placing objects on canvas, playing with the shadows and light, and creating the focal point. The fun really begins as I mix colors to come up with a palette. It's all a learning process that takes time. Why would anyone criticize my work before it's complete? So, why would I evaluate or come to conclusions about another person who is struggling to live out their dreams and "paint their life"?

I don't always get it right and have thrown out numerous paintings or repainted over existing ones—even this is part of the process. I often hang a painting in my kitchen so I can observe it over time, deciding whether or not it's finished yet. To be a painter, I've discovered I have to continue to pick up a paintbrush and begin again, recognizing mistakes or things I want to improve. No one can paint for me, and it can be painful when I receive correction or criticism (especially if unsolicited). In the end, I have to be true to what's beautiful in my own eyes and not feel diminished by the critiques of others, but rather lean in to listen and learn. Even in this book, there are paintings I did years ago that I now see problems in and ways I could improve them. However, if I spent my time correcting, criticizing, judging, and redoing each painting, I wouldn't move forward. I'd be "locked" out of the potential of creating new works of art.

I think we *should* (last one, I promise!) assume we are all on a quest to live our lives well. We're all in different stages of "becoming." None of us arrive at our destination before we begin. When we are traveling toward that destination, there may be detours or even a decision to go someplace else. I can't lock somebody in the box of my beliefs or my opinions, but instead I *should* (okay maybe a couple more) let people come to their own conclusions about what's essential in life. Each of us is becoming beautiful with time, but that beauty is subjective and looks different in everyone; it may not be the kind of art you or I appreciate. Just as everyone has different tastes in art, we all have different tastes of the heart.

If you're one of those people I have *shoulded* on, please forgive me for the guilt or judgment you may have felt from me. Please know that in no small measure, I am still in process and discovery. I hope we will all become more confident and sure of our work, accepting or rejecting the help offered along the way. Hopefully, one day we will all reach our destinations and finish our paintings.

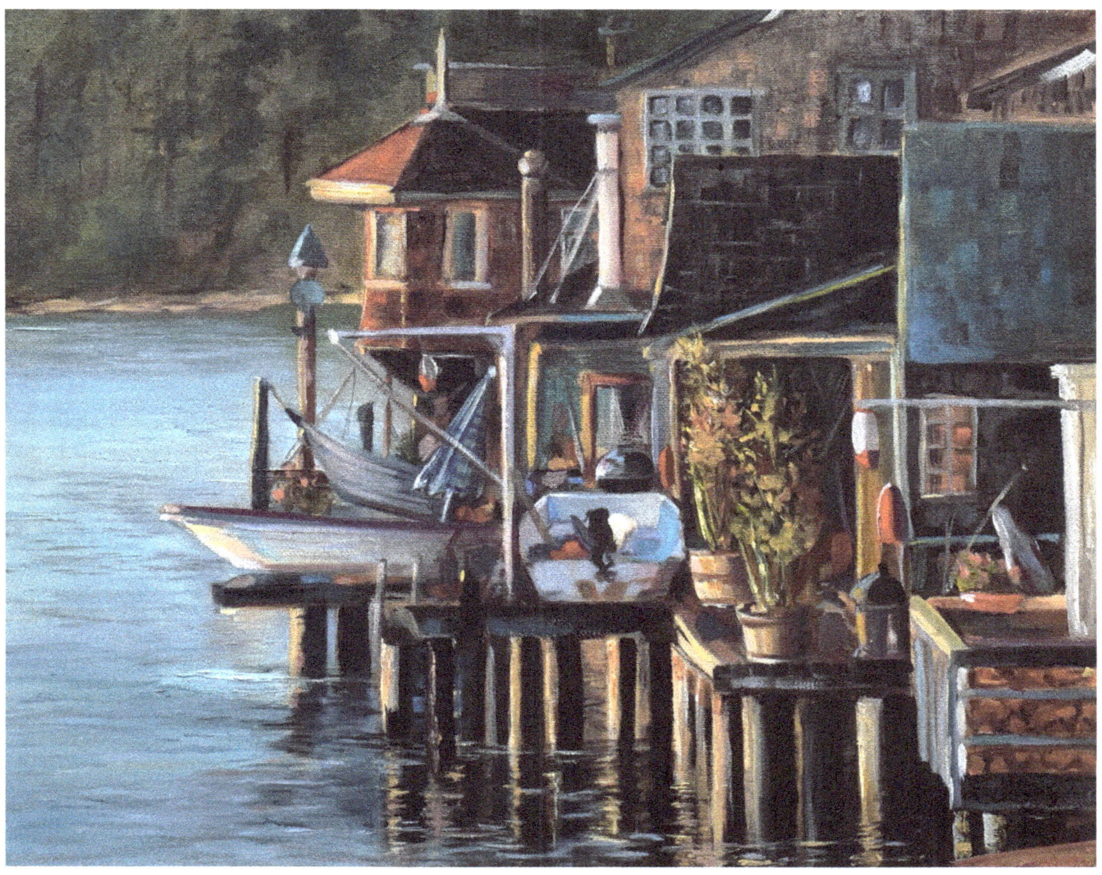

OIL PAINTING, *HANGING OUT* © 1999 LEIGH D. FITZ; WRITING, 2020

Hanging out at Salmon Beach

Hanging out at our place on Salmon Beach always felt magical, as if time slipped comfortably into an easy chair without a thought of getting up anytime soon. It was a place with nothing to achieve but to show up and take deep breaths of the cold salt air, letting our eyes feast on the beauty of the Puget Sound and the backdrop of the Olympic mountains. Salmon Beach was a place where time would stop long enough to slowly walk into its embrace and be held. When I was there, it was impossible not to smile. It was our escape—only ten minutes from our home, but a million miles away.

Our girls were in college, and our son was only ten when we purchased our property there—a rustic cabin set on pilings so that when the tide was high, our new home away from home felt like a secured houseboat. To get there, we had to leave our car behind at the top of the hill and climb down the two hundred steps to our front door. We purchased it from friends who passed this magical world on to us fully furnished, with dishes in the kitchen and sheets and blankets on the beds. Two weathered Adirondack chairs sat on the edge of the railing-less deck, beckoning us to come and take a seat.

Spending summer days and evenings hanging out at Salmon Beach afforded us time to kick back, listen to seagulls and to each other, watch the fish jump, and be mesmerized by the sunsets. These long evenings always left me with a sense that everything was all right, even when it wasn't. As I said, it was a magical place. This tiny rustic cabin held treasures of unhurried bits of conversation filled with run-on sentences that didn't require a concluding paragraph—just momentary thoughts or memories revisited, laced with satisfying chuckles, sighs, or an acknowledging glance. It was a place where honest words were untied from our controlled selves, and forgiveness was given without asking.

You can see by the painting that these cabins were close together, with a disheveled beauty. We made good friends there, who, like us, felt privileged to be on the water. Most of our cabins were humble abodes, seemingly never finished and in a constant state of disrepair.

Our son, Michael, fished from the deck during high tide and often jumped into the freezing water, a ten to fifteen-foot plunge (depending on the tides) —despite my worried words of caution. Since the deck lacked railings, he liked to get a running start for his polar plunges. One time he even brought his old bike down and rode it right off the deck! We helped him buy a little Livingston rowboat and purchased an electric motor that gave him control of the boat in the currents as he fished. However, to his great disappointment, he couldn't go faster than five miles per hour.

Summers in the Pacific Northwest, especially on the water, have cold nights where the temperature often drops into the fifties or below. Our cabin didn't have heat except for a wood-burning stove, so we would make a fire, light candles, and huddle together on our very comfortable couch. Michael always wanted to be in the middle, and he loved telling and listening to stories in the dark. I noticed back then it always seemed more natural to be ourselves in candlelight. During those times, Michael was freer to share the fears and secrets locked in his heart. There weren't electronics to draw him away from that circle of family (except an old Super Nintendo hooked up to an ancient TV that came with the cabin). I hold those tidbits of effortless conversation tenderly in my mind. Michael loved Salmon Beach as much as we did. He slept deeply there (which wasn't the case at home). We all did. It was a safe place.

I believe Salmon Beach was a saving grace for our marriage. We spent time there during some of the busiest and most stressful years of our lives, when JD's career in medicine kept him working endless hours, and when I was struggling with my own "demons" of tinnitus, migraines, and hearing loss. Salmon Beach afforded us both a sigh of relief and time to step away from the challenges we faced in real life and focus on us. It felt like we could leave the tension and stress of life in the parking lot high above the cabin, giving us a "time out" to love each other well and be grateful for God's amazing creation.

We owned our cabin on Salmon Beach for sixteen years. The kids grew up and moved away. Work eased up and escapes weren't needed anymore. We simplified life by selling the cabin. The new owners did not want anything to be left in the house, so our friends and family came and took what was valuable to them. It was so fun to see cherished objects passed on to new homes. I thought it was going to be difficult, and it was, but when we sold the cabin we didn't sell the memories. We were grateful for what this haven provided. This sad exit from the beach became a wonderful entrance to our neighborhood—affording us time to spend with neighbors and deepen our friendships in our community.

I painted the view from our deck, looking up the beach toward the northern cabins at sundown, to remind us of those moments in time when we experienced the magic of hanging out at Salmon Beach.

"He who made the Pleiades and Orion, who turns midnight into dawn and darkens day into night, who calls for the waters of the sea and pours them out over the face of the land—the Lord is his name."
Amos 5:8 (NIV)

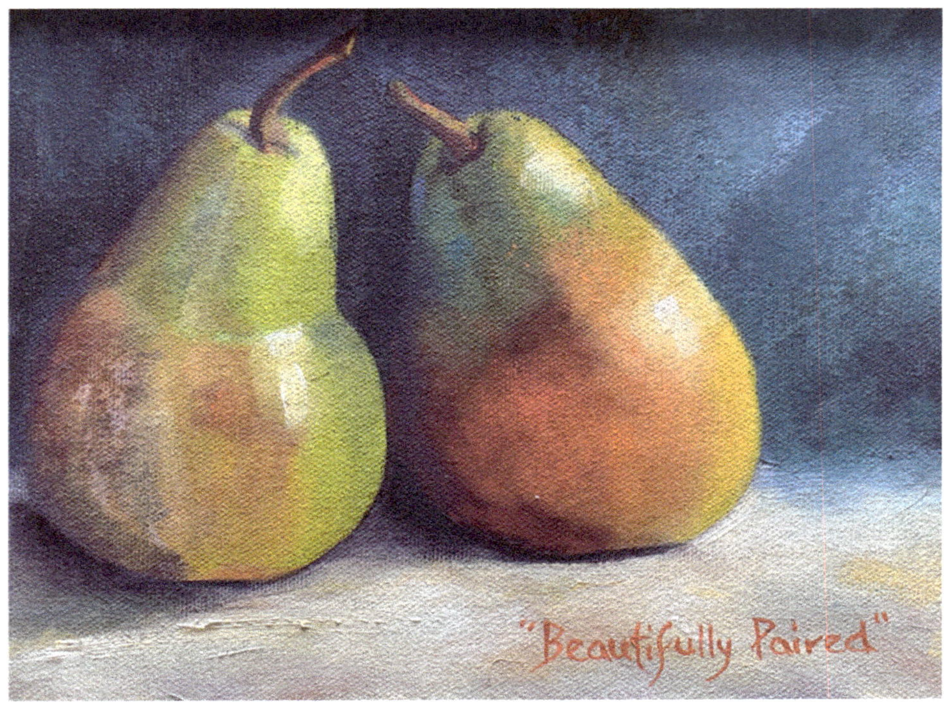

OIL PAINTING, BEAUTIFULLY PAIRED © 2012 LEIGH D. FITZ; WRITING, 2012

Beautifully Paired

Pears are tricky when it comes to judging their ripeness. Finding a ripe pear at a moment's notice is difficult at best. So, planning is essential if you want to use one in a recipe. It's one of my favorite fruits, but I've always found it challenging to find one both ideally firm and sweet. But if you do happen to capture both at just the right moment, it is a divine treat.

Relationships can be that way as well. Conversations can be tricky, and sometimes they need to be planned to have the perfect texture and sweetness—only then will there be a "ripe" conversation.

This painting started as an experiment with color and composition. In the end, the composition felt wrong. I placed the pears too high on the canvas, but the imperfection of it spoke to me about my marriage. I have learned that there are no perfect paintings nor marriages—they are all slightly "off-center." What I do love about this painting is the reminder to keep deciding to "lean in" to each other, no matter how rough it may become. I gave this little painting to JD as a thirty-eighth wedding anniversary gift with the following writing attached:

"Thirty-eight years of being married to JD Fitz has been an exciting journey. Our pairing wasn't perfect to begin with. We were unripe, and our words for each other were not always tasty. Like any couple, we've had to learn to communicate in a way we could 'hear' each other. We've learned, for instance, that ten o'clock at night is not a good time to start an emotionally charged discussion and being right or winning doesn't mean anything has been resolved.

After thirty-eight years, there are many things I can still count on: he still tells me I'm beautiful and that he's the luckiest guy being married to me. What I can't count on is whether he'll remember to pick up his dirty socks or clean up his area of the bathroom, but he won't forget to say, 'I love you,' at night before we go to sleep.

We've put in a lot of miles walking together over the years, whether it's around the block or around the world. We have biked, skied, hiked, played games, read books side-by-side, planted gardens, restored homes, worked with kids of all ages, hosted dinner parties and gatherings, attended church, and have taken classes on marriage and parenting. Almost every year of our marriage, we've gone away for a few days, just the two of us, to focus on each other and think about our goals for the future and whether our relationship was on the right track.

Over the years, we've become great friends. At present, I think we'd both say without hesitation that we are each other's best friend (which hasn't always been the case!). There's no one I'd rather be with, and I have some pretty incredible friends. JD knows me; he gets me; there's nothing hidden. We have shared our honest selves, admitted our mistakes, sins, and regrets—which, though challenging, is very freeing. We still love each other despite our flaws.

I love this man of mine. We don't have a perfect marriage; aggravations and arguments still find their way into our home. Pain still happens, and forgiveness still needs to be asked for, but at the end of the day, I can say quite honestly there's absolutely no one I'd rather be paired with. Maybe even more importantly, at the end of this thirty-eighth year of marriage, I eagerly 'lean into' the thirty-ninth year ahead. With all the titles I could have on either end of my name, I'm eternally grateful the beginning of my name is a Mrs., and at the end is Fitz. The Leigh in the middle is one happy woman!"

*"Let your speech always be gracious, seasoned with salt, so that you may know
how you want to answer each person."*
(Colossians 4:6, ESV)

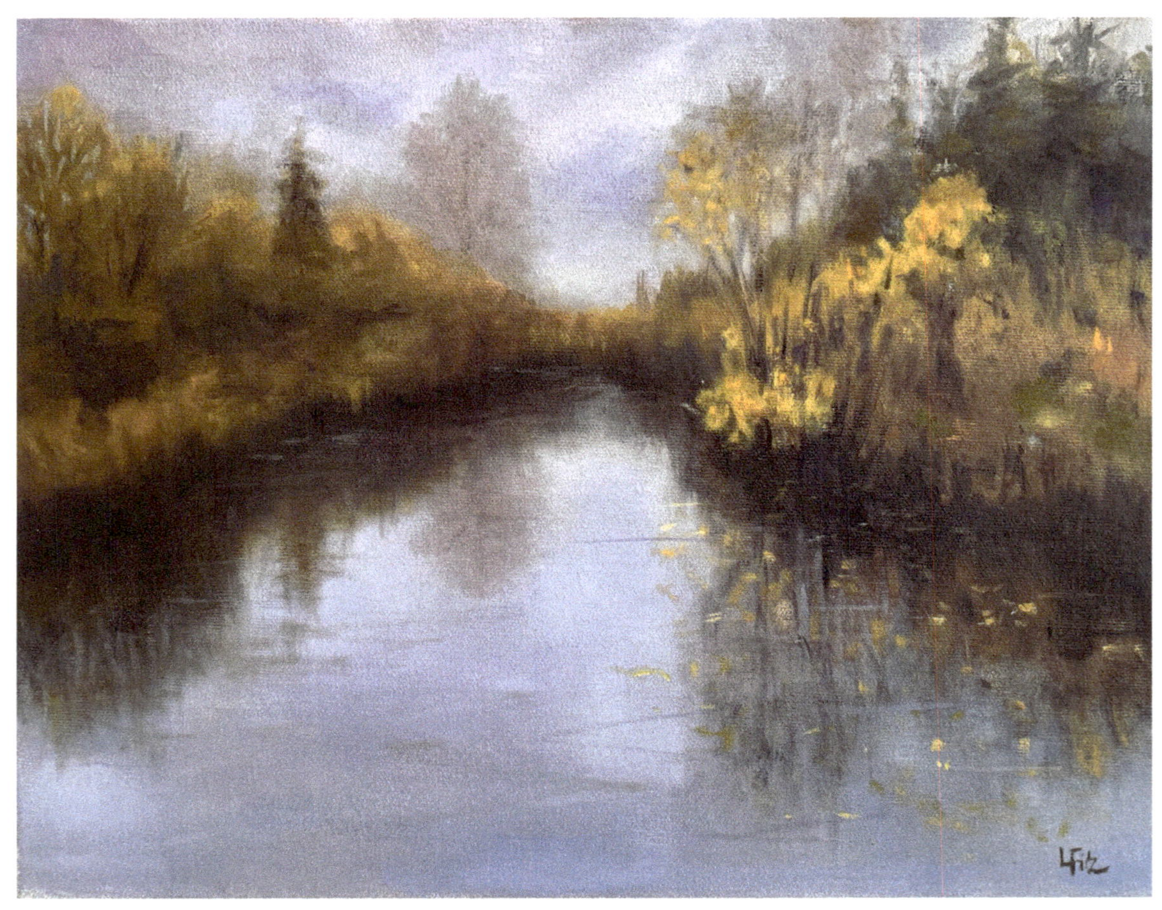

OIL PAINTING, *LAST LOOK* © 2020 LEIGH D. FITZ

Autumns

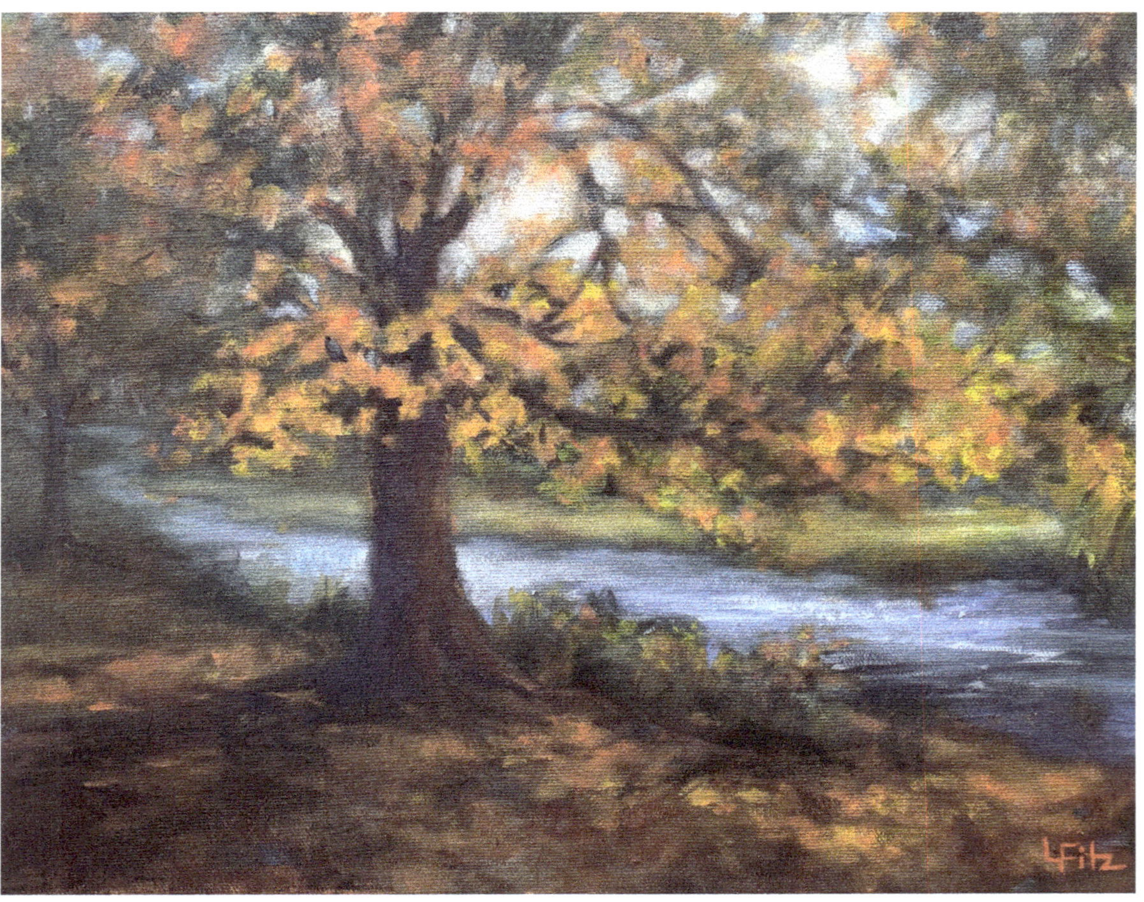

OIL PAINTING, *PLANTED* © 2016 LEIGH D. FITZ; WRITING, 2020

A Defining Moment

I believe our strongest and longest-lasting memories stem from intensely positive or negative experiences. The rest fade away because they just weren't memorable enough. Over time, these experiences we carry in our memories shape us and bring perspective to how we think and feel about ourselves and the people with whom we share our lives.

My memories of childhood are scattered, but some are crystal clear messages, as if from yesterday. I waiver over the value of going back in time to recall the child I once was. I hesitate because every time I visit her, I leave in tears. I realize, though, that it's not going back at all, but merely re-examining those weighty memories that I've been carrying for so long. It's time to lay those down.

Even now, as I broach the subject, I feel like I'm a kid again, standing in the doorway to my childhood, unable to move, unsure whether I should go in. *Will this help? Will this bring me peace? Or only more tears? I'm not sure.* So I take my child self's hand, and assure her that this time, my adult self will accompany her so there won't be anything to fear. I tell her, "We won't only visit the harsh words spoken, but also the kind words that were dispensed, even if the doses seemed small." Come along if you like—you may see yourself, too, in some aspects of my life.

As I enter the classroom, I can see my second-grade self, a skinny little girl with a pixie cut and a cowlick that is sticking straight up. Her head droops in dread as she drags her chair behind her to the front of the room, where her teacher is sitting in a big blue wicker chair. Mrs. Bacchus has wiry, graying hair, wrinkles, and a face frozen in a scowl, never generous with smiles. She tells this child she's not good enough to be in a reading group. Instead, the girl has to endure the humiliation of reading out loud to the teacher in front of the class.

The class is supposed to be working while the teacher reads with her, but what they're doing instead is snickering at her attempts at reading, and at every mistake she makes. She's already missed the word "oh" a couple times, calling it "ho" instead. (She has dyslexia, but nobody knows that yet, especially not Mrs. Bacchus.)

When the word comes again, two sentences later, she misses it for the third time. At this point, Mrs. Bacchus, in her frustration, erupts into a rage as she pounds the book repeatedly with her finger, yelling, "The word is oh, O - H; why can't you get it?! You stupid, stupid girl!" The sound of laughter erupts as well, as Mrs. Bacchus sends the girl to the cloakroom for punishment. Shame and tears are with her as she leaves. Nobody knows that the little girl will carry the weight of the word "stupid" for the rest of her life. She will allow it to define her and convince her of her worthlessness.

I see the same girl painting a picture of trees in the art class down the hall. Her art teacher notices it and thinks it's incredible. She compliments the girl as she accompanies her back to class with the painting in hand to show to Mrs. Bacchus, telling her that, for a second grader, it's really quite impressive. I wish that little girl could've allowed those words to accompany her as well through life, but by then, I think she was deaf to words of encouragement. The negative words in her head yelled too loudly for the soft-spoken, positive ones to be heard.

To this day, words still trip me up and have become my nemesis. Even as an adult, I do all sorts of crazy things with my words: mispronouncing them, failing to remember their meaning, creatively misspelling them, or forgetting the word I want to say right in the middle of my sentence!

I remember other words I was given in third grade, words I memorized. I don't know the teacher's name. I can no longer see his face, but he taught a class on Wednesday nights at our church. Through pictures on a flannel board, he encouraged us, with smiles and treats, to memorize Psalm 1 out of the Bible: "Blessed is the man who does not walk in the counsel of the ungodly, nor stands in the way of sinners, nor sits in the seat of the scoffers. But his delight is in the law of the Lord, and on it, he meditates day and night. He is like a tree planted by the rivers of water, which brings forth fruit in season. His leaf does not wither, and whatever he did, he prospers."[7]

Those verses spoke of hope. Those words told me I had a chance; I could even prosper! Those words had pictures I could comprehend, so I slipped them into the pocket of my memory and often took them out to whisper aloud. The teacher also told us that God loved us, and I hoped that included me as well, even if I was "stupid." God was going to grow me like a healthy tree and help me to bear fruit!

This psalm has accompanied me through my life, reminding me that taking the time to talk to God each day is helpful. He wanted me to listen to His words, not the mocking ones in my head. Those verses gave me a way to pray to God. I began asking for His help. (I do recollect imploring Him to come and get me so that I would never have to go to school again, but when that didn't happen, I devised ways to feign sickness by putting the thermometer on the radiator when my mom wasn't looking.)

This is what I've concluded from my experience: how we dispense words is vitally important, especially to young kids. It is critical to the growth of those who receive our words. They have the potential to bring life or death, to tenderly love or critically demean, to help children grow healthy in mind or ruin their view of themselves. Children are like young saplings that need extra care in their planting, watering, pruning, and staking, to nourish their growth process and lead healthy lives.

I've also learned that visiting the defining moments of our lives and our memories from the past, as tough as they may be, can provide insight into the way we define ourselves today. It's made me notice my pencil has an eraser—and I'm thinking of using it on the word "stupid" and writing the word "creative" instead!

7. Psalm 1:1-2, ESV

Post Script:

Recently I reconnected and had a three-hour conversation with the woman who was my best friend in grade school. We hadn't talked for over forty years. We reflected together on second grade and Mrs. Bacchus and how mean she was to me. This friend was a witness to my life back then. She called Mrs. Bacchus' behavior toward me "child abuse."

We discussed and reminisced about all the fun we had growing up, recalling the times of laughter and our two very creative selves playing and making up stories, dressing up in my mother's old gowns, dividing up and rearranging dollhouse furniture, all the candy we ate, and our mothers and how good they were to us. We also reviewed our childhood faith in God, getting the giggles in church and how both of us still love Jesus today. As we were saying goodbye, my friend said, " . . . and Leigh, I love you!"

I let those words seep down into my little girl's heart and like a salve, cover the wounds of abuse that were inflicted on me from an unkind old woman. Healing has come. Her words swiftly altered my second-grade year into something remarkably wonderful. I'm grateful I had a friend who, despite my struggles in school, loved me just the way I was. Now that little girl emerges once again, back out of the door of childhood, with tears streaming down her cheeks—but this time they are tears of joy! (Thank you, Michelle; I love you too!)

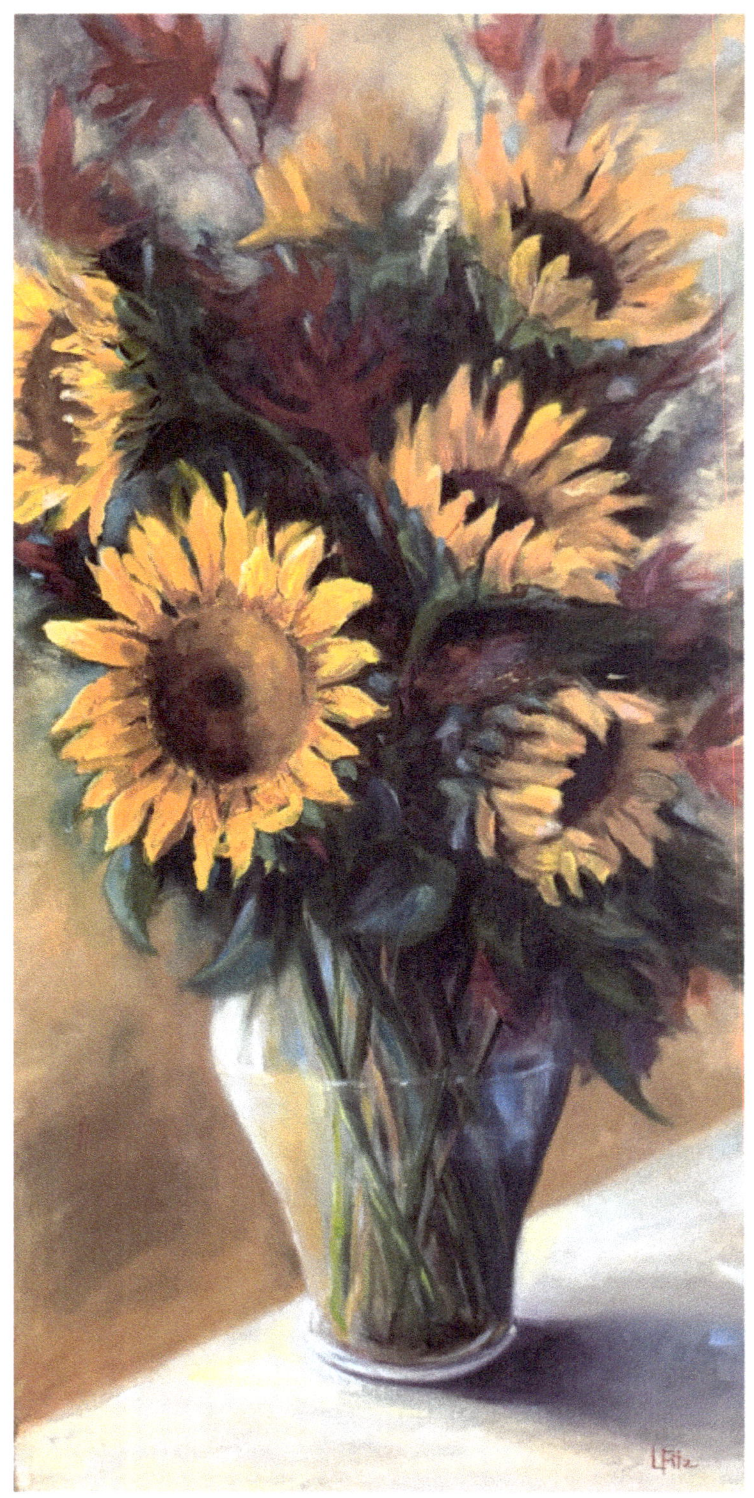

OIL PAINTING, *BEST DRESSED,* © 2009 LEIGH D. FITZ; WRITING, 2019

Clothes that Never Go out of Style

Sunflowers, to me, feel bold and wild—they are a happy flower. Greeting them always stirs up joy in my heart. I've read that, as they grow, the blossoms turn toward the sun.

After buying some sunflowers at our local Saturday morning farmer's market, I came home and arranged them on my front porch with maple branches that had turned bright red with autumn. They were for a friend's mother's funeral, and sunflowers had been her favorite. Just as I was about to take them into the house, the sun hit the flowers, radiating their glory and beauty. I snapped a few pictures so I could paint them at another time. Flowers always look so fabulous when "dressed" in sunshine!

Sometimes getting dressed in the morning can be an ordeal for me—no matter where I'm going or what the occasion, I aim to look my best. I want my make up to be applied tastefully. I care about what I look like in public and, frankly, even when I'm home. I inherited this trait from my mother, who cared a great deal about her clothes and the outward appearance of her three teenage daughters as we grew up in Southern California. She would give us the once over whenever we left the house. She noticed what we were wearing, how much makeup we had applied, and whether our hair was coiffed just right. If something was amiss or not up to her expectations, we were sent back to our room to change. We were not told that we were pretty but instead to, "Go put your face on," or, "That color isn't right for you," or, "That makes you look fat." I assumed the best compliment from her was no words at all.

Living in the Pacific Northwest, where Birkenstocks and fleece jackets abound, has freed me to choose my clothes with less self-judgment and has undoubtedly altered my outward appearance. But I still hear my mother's voice in my head, urging me to "look my best." So, if I'm honest, when I get ready for an event, I agonize too much over what I'm going to wear. I wonder what other people will be wearing. I want to fit in, look my best, and be pretty. I want to be seen as somebody that has style. But a Bible verse I read recently stopped me in my tracks and made me reconsider my clothing style: "Therefore, as God's chosen people, holy and dearly loved, *clothe yourselves* with compassion, kindness, humility, gentleness, and patience."[8]

8. Colossians 3:12, NIV, emphasis added

Now, there's nothing wrong with looking my best, but this verse got me thinking and asking myself how I get "dressed." *How do I prepare or "dress" my mind, heart, or emotions? How do I clothe myself with "compassion" as I start each day? How do I get ready for the conversations that will occur? Who are the people I'm going to see?*

And what kind of frame of mind are they in? Are they struggling? What are some kind, encouraging words I can say? Is my compassion toward others as soft as my cashmere sweater? Am I first choosing to clothe myself with worldly goods or the apparel of kindness? Do I care more about the covering of kindness or the style of my jeans? I'm learning that the colors of kindness are far more complimentary. And, speaking of compliments, do I care more about being complimented on my clothes or the person I'm becoming? Or, should I even think about being complimented at all?

Is there gentleness in my voice as I give my words away? Gentleness seems more important than whether I have the perfect boots to match my outfit. I want to be gentle, especially in these times when this world feels fragile and people are hurting.

How do I slip on humility each day? My humility clothes remind me that I don't have to wear the latest trend. Humility looks good on everyone. C.S. Lewis said, "True humility is not thinking less of yourself; it is thinking of yourself less." If this statement is true, then I have work to do.

I've also noticed that these kinds of clothes, especially kindness and compassion, are not quickly "put on." In my attempt to keep putting them on daily, I memorized this verse from Colossians and tried to remember to say it to myself while getting dressed in the morning or for an event, but it wasn't long-lived. Then I decided to make a sign with this verse on it to put in my closet, but honestly, the sign isn't finished yet. Conjuring up heaps of gentleness and patience is not as easily accomplished as getting dressed. These "clothes" are not available on Amazon Prime nor can I find them at stores near me.

So, today, I'm asking the only One who can help me. I'm asking God to give me greater compassion for people—to provide ideas on how to act with kindness toward my family and anyone I happen to run into each day. I'm asking the only resource capable, God Himself, to dress me in compassion, kindness, humility, gentleness, and patience. I ask Him to tell me if these clothes already exist in my closet, and if so, to help me learn to no longer ignore them as clothing choices. And finally, I ask Him to help keep these clothes washed and ready to wear as I engage with my husband, family members, and our community. Also, disrobing from my clothing of pride, envy, and discontent would be helpful. They need to bypass Goodwill and go directly into the garbage once and for all!

Clothes can be a beautiful veneer, and perhaps they help to impress quickly, but after a few conversations, the heart of a person emerges. I hope and pray when my heart appears to others it will be far more attractive than the clothes I'm wearing. Kindness, compassion, humility, gentleness, and patience, never go out of style; they look fabulous on everyone!

"Lord, I want to wear You well today." ~ Mary Howe

"And why do you worry about clothes? See how the flowers of the field grow.
They do not labor or spin. Yet I tell you that not even Solomon in all his splendor
was dressed like one of these. If that is how God clothes the grass of the field,
which is here today and tomorrow is thrown into the fire,
will he not much more clothe you—you of little faith?"
(Matthew 6:28–30, NIV)

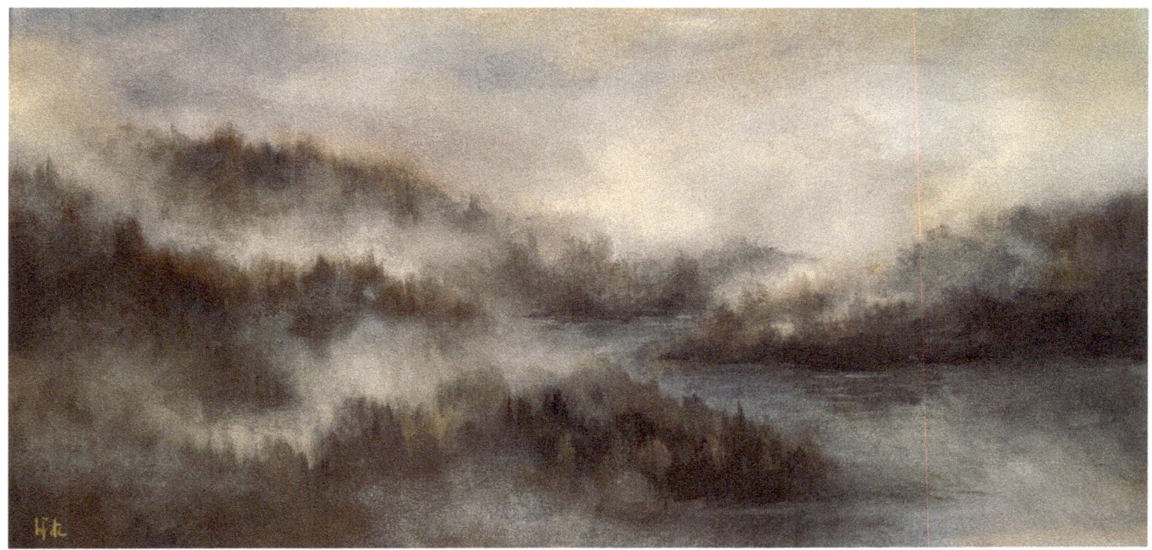

OIL PAINTING, *NATURE'S LAMENT* © 2020 LEIGH D. FITZ; WRITING, 2020

Nature's Lament

When the weather mirrors my sorrow with gentle rain, I'm grateful. It's as if nature is being empathetic. Fog roams quietly through pine, silently watering the trees as if it doesn't want to interrupt, honoring a solemn moment of grief.

I have come to the belief that weeping over loss isn't wrong; it's essential. Time may heal wounds, but somehow I never let the memory slip entirely from my grasp. Grief is inconvenient and demands my attention—never caring if I'm exhausted. It shows up uninvited and stays longer than I would have liked.

Grieving over loss does not nullify nor diminish my trust in God; rather, it enhances it. When life is breaking off pieces of my heart that already feel dry and cracked, God sees me, but, at times, I have difficulty seeing Him. When grief catches me off guard, I find myself "pounding the chest of God" with questions or anger, moaning, or drenching a bed with tears of sadness. The heart laments over its fractured state, unsure how it can be mended and crying out to God with indistinct mutterings. Though I may not feel His arms of comfort, I know that God is holding me as He weeps as well. His tears, full of grace, seep down deep, touching my wounds of worry, replenishing my heart with His endless supply of comfort. He understands the sadness, is acquainted with grief, and wants to sit with me so we can mourn together. I believe He does this with you as well. Tears in the presence of God, tears of hurt, pain, or sorrow, feel like a form of prayer—a lament. This wordless interaction causes a mysterious closeness to God, allowing sorrow to be held by His tender arms of understanding. A truthful abiding.

I have journeyed with close girlfriends who have experienced horrific losses that I can't even begin to fathom. I have stood beside them at graves, made flower arrangements to spread over caskets, and attempted to dispense healing words, but who other than God can tenderly embrace the soul of a person and understand their pain fully? Over the years, I've seen in their loss the quiet resolve to keep trusting God even when life turns pitch black. It's been an honor for me to be a witness to their lives as they have walked through steep valleys of shadows and death, emerging full of both wisdom and compassion as they effectively comfort others in need.

How, Lord, can I be thankful in the midst of sorrow? Walking out into the sun-filled day with a smile on my face feels phony when my heart aches. I'm not sure I will "get over" loss, but I will get on with it. Today, I will attempt to make a space for gratefulness to sit alongside my sorrow. I'm longing for the day when the fog lifts, tears and sorrow cease to exist, and I'm turned forever toward the Light.

"We don't yet see things. We're squinting in a fog, peering through a mist.
But it won't be long before the weather clears and the sun shines bright! We'll see it all then, see it all as clearly
as God sees us, knowing Him directly just as He knows us!"
(1 Corinthians 13:12, MSG)

"Praise be to the God and father of our Lord Jesus Christ, the father of compassion
and the God of all comfort, who comforts us in all our troubles,
so that we can comfort those in any trouble with the comfort
we ourselves have received from God."
(2 Corinthians 1:3-4, NIV)

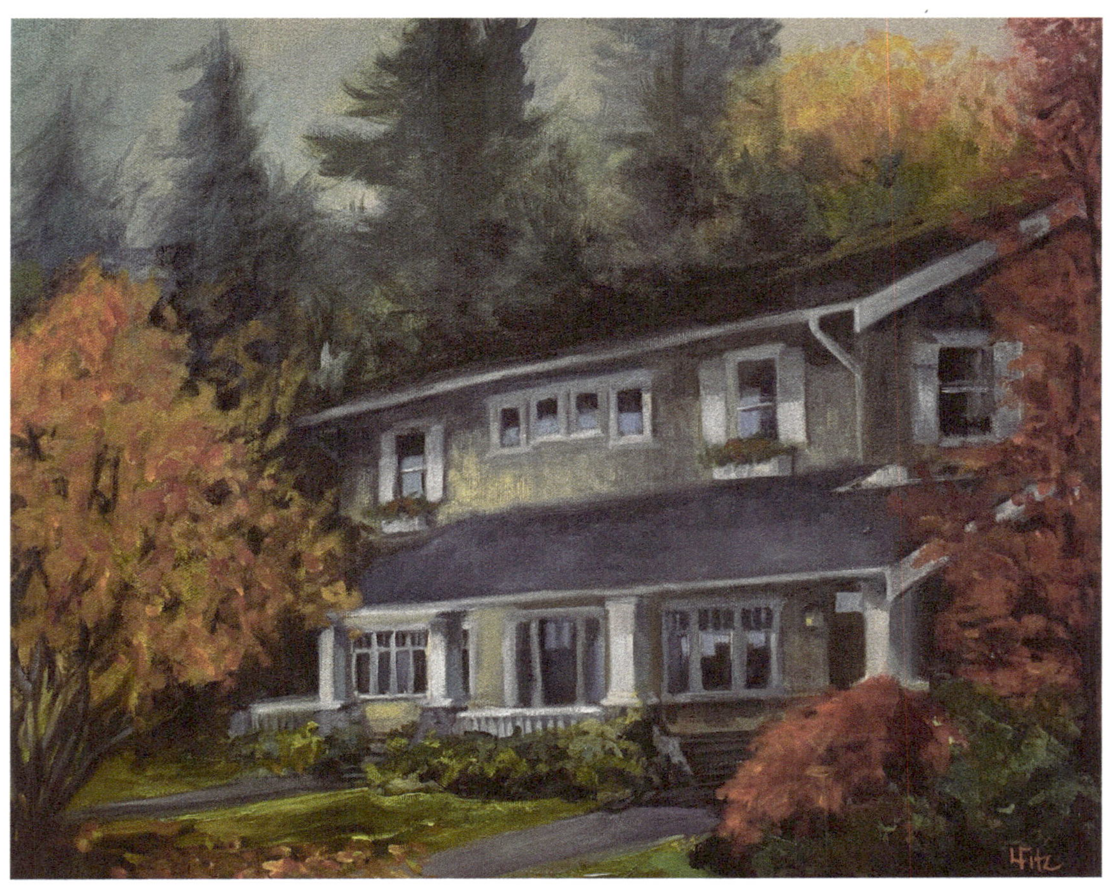

OIL PAINTING, *THE HOUSE THAT HOLDS MY HOME,* © 2004 LEIGH D. FITZ; WRITING, 2012

The House that Holds My Home

(Journal entry from May 2012)

My oldest daughter, Anne, and her family moved in with us last Sunday; they will be here three and a half months while their own house is being built. Two women under one roof isn't always easy. We both are still in the polite stage, attempting not to get in each other's space too much, but we do have to share the kitchen, eating area, and the family room. I feel as though my house has been invaded, and it is my home. Right?

Well, this morning, I was discussing the situation and my frustrations with God when I remembered (or maybe He was the one who brought it up) that this house belongs to Him, and He's letting me live here. It's incredible how a little shift in my mind can transform my attitude.

I had been asking God for His assistance on loving others with His love, but I've been so focused on my house lately—the way my things are being dirtied, scratched, and filled with unfamiliar objects and noise, with a bit of chaos on the side—that I don't feel like loving or sharing. I want my toys (my house) back! And once again, I realize my shortcomings and my need to give and genuinely love people more than things. My God knows exactly what to do with these filthy rags of fret and complaint I'm handing Him. (It's so nice to have house help!)

A month into this experience, with my attitude finally on the right track (so I thought), my son-in-law Eric spilled a glass of red wine all over a white chair. Needless to say, I wasn't too happy, and it was difficult to hide my frustration or control my attitude. Accidents happen. In hindsight, though, I'm grateful for the spill, the valuable lesson it taught me, and the question that floated through my mind that night a few hours later.

What matters most to you, Leigh, your white chair or your son-in-law? Because right now, it looks like the chair is winning your favor! I remember walking back downstairs into our family room, where he was on his knees, still working on the stain (which did come out, by the way). When he looked up at me, I saw the agony in his eyes, pleading for my forgiveness. And I realized, once again, in that moment, how deeply I loved him and how difficult this whole situation was for him to not only be living in my home, but to have to go through this experience of regret and sorrow for spilling wine.

Compassion was freshly born in me that night. I was the one who needed forgiveness. I had let my frustrations "spill" out on him, leaving him "stained" emotionally by my fussing over a chair instead of loving and caring about his feelings. I assured him that I loved him more than any object in my house, and I meant it.

(Journal entry from September 2012)

As fall arrives, this dear family has just left to move into their new home. Tears come to my eyes, thinking about how much I gained in having them here and how sad I am to see them go. They filled the house with life through their voices and activities. My kitchen table was in continuous use serving endless meals and snacks. At all times of the day and night, it was a spot for dialogues and debates, board games, playing cards, computers, paperwork, and a myriad of art projects. It was a summer of laughter, cuddles with my grandkids, reading stories together, playing hide and seek, running through sprinklers, and jumping in the hot tub—enjoying the rhythm of life. Now it will be silent.

I know I won't miss the crumbs, mishaps, spills, fingerprints, my constant attempts at cleaning up or, bringing order to the chaos, or our very full, disorganized refrigerator, but I will miss seeing each face around the table at dinner time, the late-night talks after the grandkids were in bed. I'll miss those moments! No more hugs whenever the kids were leaving the house or coming home. (My one rule that I insisted on turned out to be my personal favorite.) The effect of my grandkids' hugs surpassed that of any mess they made! They brought huge amounts of joy into this house.

The long walks and talks with Anne have been wonderful. Both she and Eric have been helpful and energetic. I will miss watching them up close as they parent their kids and love each other. They do a great job of it! I have loved watching my daughter be a wife and mom! I'm proud of her. The four of us and our two grandkids have all grown close. I've gleaned wisdom from each one. The secure bond we share at this point, I fear, will dwindle with time but I am grateful we had it this summer.

Through it all, I never heard a complaint; there were no arguments. I'm sure they were frustrated being crammed into a basement for three and a half months, under my watchful eye, with little privacy, but they handled it well. I think we all did.

Was I relieved to get my house back? Well, honestly yes, but the loss of them no longer living in our town, not being able to go for a walk with my daughter on a moment's notice, not eating at each other's homes, not having the constant hugs and hearing the daily, "I love you, Nana," are all killers to my heart, none of which I will soon forget.

Gone are the toys, crumbs, multiple phones, iPads, computers, numerous cords, purses, keys, wallets and "stuff" everywhere. But what will remain are the memories of the summer we spent living together as a family under one roof. I refuse to let them take those memories with them. I will clutch them to my heart and hold them close for many years to come. And, okay, here come the tears once again.

(Journal entry from 2020)

Yes, that summer we shared our home was crazy, fun, and wonderful! Our two families collided, and we became closer on so many levels. This morning these memories came flooding back as I accidentally spilled hot tea, drenching the arm of my fairly new white chair, and felt that gut-punch of regret, wishing I could rewind my actions. *Eric, I feel your pain, but I'm not going to beat myself up because I've learned that people are more important than a chair. Thanks for the lesson you taught me!*

This painting is like my life. It's far from perfect, with imperfectly straight lines, and perhaps lacking in perspective, but at a glance, it fills me with thirty years' worth of abundant memories. This is the home where I raised my kids and watch my grandkids grow. Every room is brimming with stories of the past, the celebrations of milestones, arguments big and small, "family hugs" that were given generously, nightly dinners around our kitchen table sharing both food and each other's lives, bedtime talks, reassurances, prayers, forgiveness, and the holiday traditions. Even the hallways echo the sounds of little feet, laughter, teasing, and music. Memories, so many memories. This house holds my heart and my love for family.

The fall color on the trees in the painting signals that change is coming. JD and I have been thinking that we probably should scale down and move to a more suitable place, just for two. It's a lot of work to tend to the 108-year-old house and its gardens. The memories in this house will be difficult to leave behind, so I'm looking for ways to pack all the remembrances and take them with me. It's scary to think of living someplace else. God knows what we need, so I keep asking Him to lead us. But one thought I recently stumbled on renewed my calm: wherever my husband and I live, I'm "at home," because he is my home! My house is merely a structure that holds my "home"—the people I love!

"By wisdom a house is built, and through understanding it is established;
through knowledge its rooms are filled with rare and beautiful treasures."
(Proverbs 24:3-4, NIV)

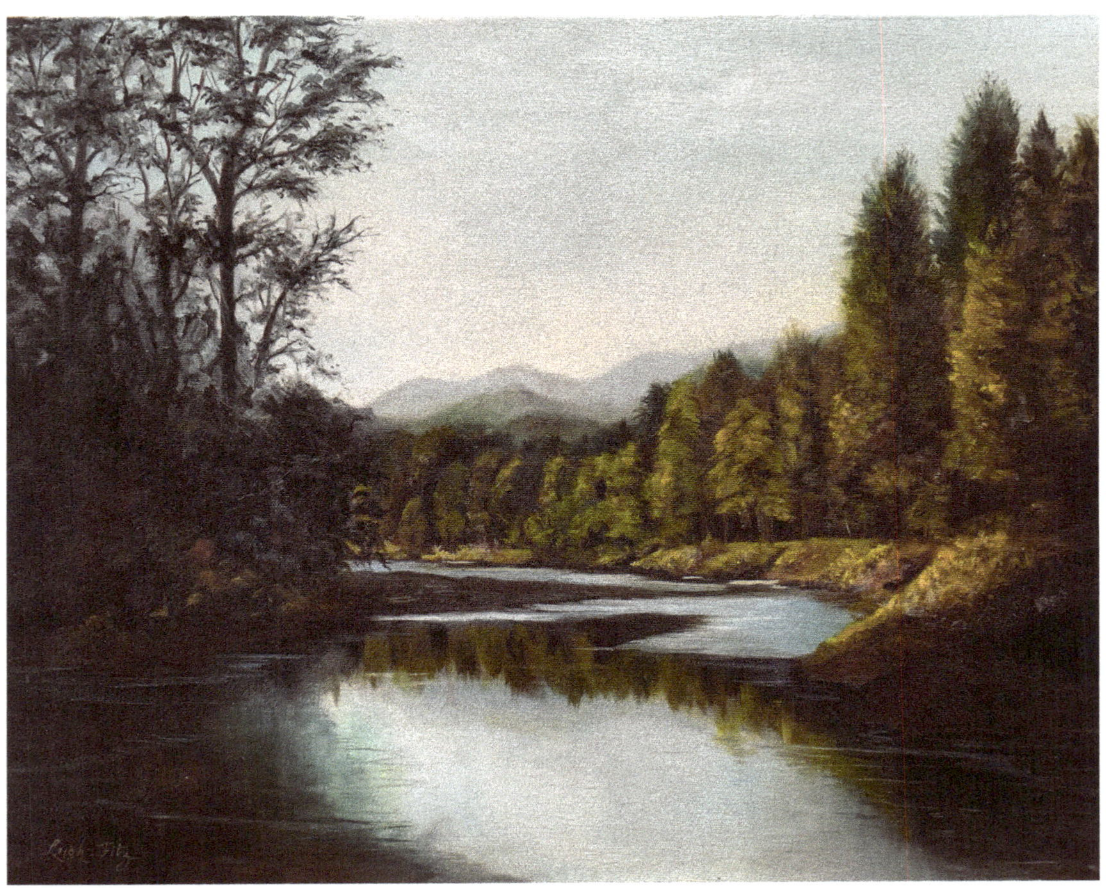

OIL PAINTING, *HOLDING MEMORIES CLOSE* © 2001 LEIGH D. FITZ; WRITING, 2001

Peace Like a River

Creating space in a relationship amidst the mundane routines of life isn't easy to achieve. The very moment I need it, I frankly don't feel like making an effort.

At the end of one particularly busy, stressful week, JD and I were driving on the Cascade Highway toward Stevens Pass in Washington State to watch Michael play football under the Friday night lights. To save time, I had packed sandwiches for dinner to eat along the way. What I hadn't anticipated was the beauty we discovered as we made our way on this winding mountain road. At one point, we couldn't resist pulling over to eat our sandwiches by the side of the Skagit River as the sun started its descent—slipping down and playing hide-and-seek among the trees. I don't recall the words spoken, but I remember the peace and contentment I felt as I snapped a few pictures.

Peace and contentment like that can be difficult for us to come by. Our days are crowded with kids, school, and sports—chock-full of the mundane rhythms of day-to-day tasks. JD's rigorous and demanding work schedule leaves little time to be alone as a couple. This evening was the typical fare, hurrying from one thing to another, not wanting to be late or miss the starting time.

But this time of stepping away from the typical to experience the extraordinary was a valuable lesson for me. By taking fifteen minutes from our schedule, we created a memory. The two of us, just sitting and eating sandwiches, watching nature, listening to the gentle movement of the water, experiencing beauty together—a long-overdue peace-filled moment. Later I captured this scene on canvas, locking in my mind the significance of being proactive in my marriage. It takes conscious effort to make the most of the little ordinary moments we do have, to "breathe in" life, making space, however small, for harmony to grow, instead of complaining or arguing about time that has already slipped from our reach. I recognize that, far too often, I can destroy the good between us by pointing to the deficiencies rather than creating margin to re-discover, remember, and be thankful for the love that binds us. This doesn't mean it solves all our problems with communication or the tension that sometimes stands between us, but it brings a healing salve to our emotions.

These moments cause me to stop and remember that there's good in this marriage, there is good in this man, and there is even good in me. A bit of mending occurs at a time when both can receive it.

Just as I take the time to capture pictures of beauty (like this river), I want to make time to take "pictures" of the goodness and beauty I see in my partner—a moment for my memory to be nudged, allowing grace and love to win the day.

"Oh, that you had paid attention to my commandments!
Then your peace would have been like a river,
and your righteousness like the waves of the sea."
(Isaiah 48:18, ESV)

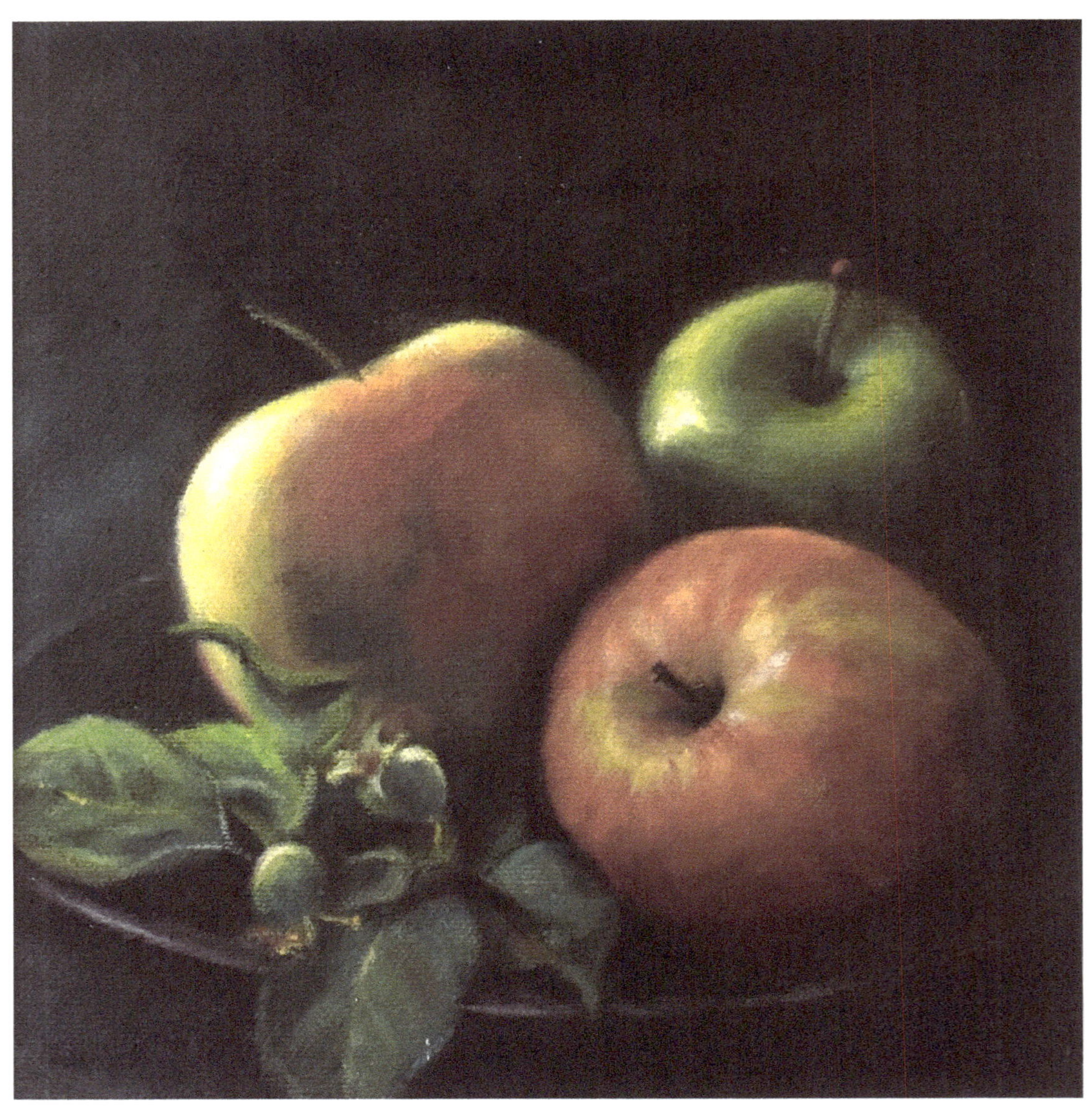

Holy Spirit Fruit

"…the fruit of the Spirit is love, joy, peace, patience, kindness,
goodness, faithfulness, gentleness, and self-control."
(Galatians 5:22-23, NIV)

Living out God's Spirit is simply not possible on my own. Try as I might, I can't conjure up love and goodness in myself. It's not sustainable. I need help. I have noticed, though, as I attempt to live by the Spirit's guidance and follow His lead in my daily life, something quite remarkable takes place. Love sprouts in a dying relationship. Joy bubbles up from within me instead of complaints. Peace rules in my mind instead of worry. Patience teaches me to take a deep breath, to summon up a more effective response, and waits with me amid frustration. Kindness cuts in front of my self-absorbed world and surprises me with its life-giving effect.

Goodness grows, and others notice a difference. Faithfulness, though only measured with time, begins multiplying. Gentleness rescues a harsh response. Suddenly my words are more tender than before. Self-control—well, self-control is a fruit that is needed every day, in every area of my life. It's controlling what comes out of my mouth or what goes in, how I spend my money or how I give it away, how I keep myself in shape or just sit on the sidelines, how I utilize my time effectively by giving to others or hoard it all for myself. It's a push/pull with the Spirit, but thankfully He is so loving and patient with me. He is kind and good. He is faithful and gentle to me daily, even when I'm running from His lead. His self-control is a testimony to His commitment and undying love for me and each of us in the everyday moments. He chose (and continues to want) me, no matter how I act. But as I watch Him work, as I listen to Him more and more, I begin to look and act like Him. He transforms me bit by bit.

Suddenly, I'm rethinking what I'm going to ask for Christmas—fruit! I want more of the Holy Spirit fruit! And I don't want just enough for me; I want to be able to share it with others who are in need as well.

Years ago, I felt led to send this piece to a struggling friend. Years later, he told me he constantly was making copies of it and passing it out in AA meetings. He spoke to me a couple of times about how he could not live without these words and repeatedly read them.

Once, when this same man went missing, my husband and I prayed for guidance to find him. I received a picture in my mind's eye of a random rundown hotel along the I-5 freeway. I identified the motel, and placed a call to the front desk and asked to speak to my friend. They transferred me to his room and he answered. When he heard my voice, he started weeping, and agreed to let us go pick him up.

His battle with alcohol was lengthy, with never-ending ups and downs, but he kept loving God through to the end. And I could see these fruits of God's spirit growing in him. This experience "ripened" the Holy Spirit fruit within me as well and taught me the value of giving away words of encouragement and listening to God's promptings.

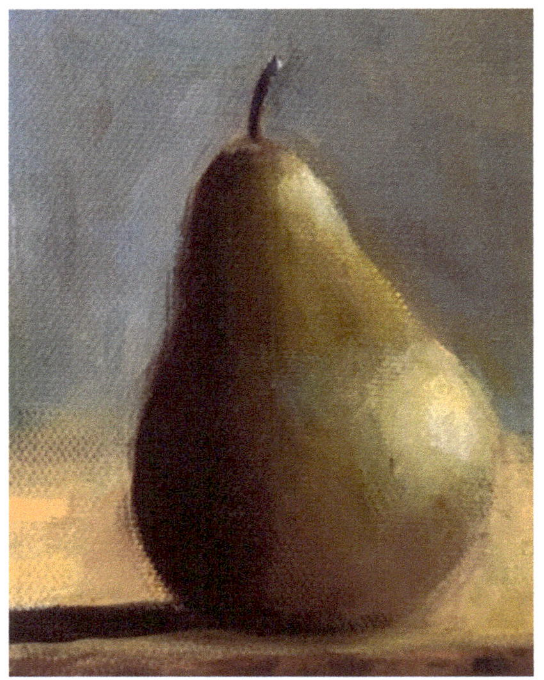

Longings

Longings. We have all probably experienced some yearning or desire that grows within our hearts. A longing to belong, to be loved, for meaning, for peace in our lives, or to have a good friend to accompany us in life.

What am I longing for at this moment? I long to be as close to God as I possibly can without changing my lifestyle too drastically! Ha! The second part of that sentence didn't arrive in my thoughts until I wrote the word "God"! But honestly, that last part rings true sometimes for me. Being close to God should have to change my lifestyle a bit, don't you think?

Is it true that we can be as close to God as we choose? The word choice means "to decide on a course of action, typically after rejecting alternatives." This implies there is a course of action I can take to become closer to God. But what does that course of action look like in everyday life? And what's *my* course of action? Well, we talk pretty regularly—but I think I do most of the talking, so listening might be useful. We meet together for tea and toast in the mornings, but I often ignore Him while I'm reading something other than what He has written, and other times I stand Him up altogether!

The Gospels seem to imply that Jesus and His disciple, John, were pretty close. In his writings, John always referred to himself as "one Jesus loved," and we read in the biblical narratives that John not only sat by Jesus but leaned on Him. Why John? What was it about him that set him apart from the other disciples? Why were he and Jesus so close, and how can I get there too?

When I was a teenager, I bought a guitar and taught myself the basic chords. I wasn't a great singer, but I loved to create songs and sing them to Jesus when I was alone. I started putting tunes to Scripture verses that I was attempting to memorize. As I think back now to those snapshots of myself trying to write songs about my love for Jesus, or singing Scripture—baring my soul and singing my heart out—*that* was leaning in. I had a longing to belong even then.

I also wondered if people liked me, and I tried to morph myself into somebody likable, even if I was going against the grain of my true self. I struggled with self-confidence in high school, but thankfully I had an amazing girlfriend, Ann (after whom I named my firstborn daughter), who rescued me from loneliness at school. She was a popular girl, cheerleader, gorgeous blonde, super-intelligent, and involved in everything. I always wondered why she befriended me.

When I was with her, I could be myself, and I liked who I was when I was with her. My grades improved in those years—I think I recognized that Ann's good grades were the product of her study habits, so I started studying too. When I was with her, I was accepted and could sit amongst her other friends at lunch with confidence, but if she were ever absent from school, I hid out in the library. Without her, I felt like I was a nobody who wanted to be somebody, but I didn't know how.

Even today, it's easy to slip into a funk, feeling that my friends are few and far between. Sometimes I feel lonely and convince myself that nobody likes me; they just put up with me. I assume everybody else is having a good time being invited over to other people's homes and being well-connected to an infinite number of friends on Facebook or other social media sites. But in my relationships with women over the years, I have found that many struggle with these same feelings of loneliness and exclusion, whether married or single.

And, BTW (by the way), it doesn't matter how close I am to my husband at any given moment; I also need my girlfriends! Without them, I would overrun him with an avalanche of words and thoughts because I have so many of them that need to be said. Having girlfriends affords me chances to download some of those words and ideas that my husband doesn't need to hear. I find my girlfriends listen and encourage differently. There is commonality and laughter. They can relate, empathize, and speak wisdom into my life. A great friend like Ann doesn't compete but cheerleads, sharing in our excitement and grieving with us in our losses.

I find the "longing to belong" begins to be fulfilled when I make the first move. It takes being a good friend to have a good friend. So, I'm thinking of ways to pursue my God—to "lean on" Him like John did. My voice isn't as clear as it was in high school, but I'm guessing God would still love me to sing Him a line or two. I'm "scooting" closer to Him and I'm picking up the phone to reach out to a friend.

———

"I will sing a new song to you, O God, on the ten-stringed lyre.
I will make music to you."
(Psalms 144:9, NIV)

"A friend loves at all times, and a brother (or sister) is born for a time of adversity."
(Proverbs 17:17, NIV)

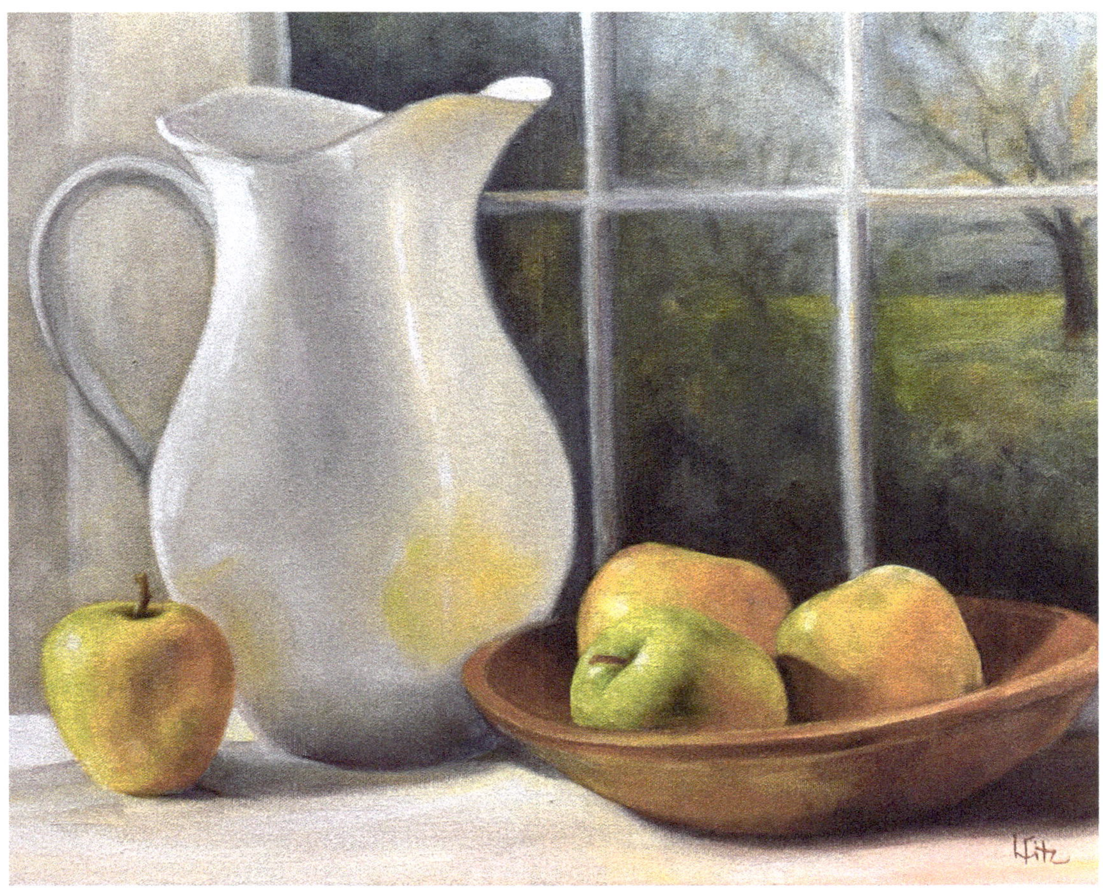

OIL PAINTING, SHEDDING LIGHT © 2016 LEIGH D. FITZ; WRITING, 2020

Shine on Me

"To light" is a phrase that once meant only "to illuminate by candlelight or firelight." But around the fifteenth century, "light" was also understood to mean "understanding." The phrase "shed light on" means to "make something less confusing or to clarify by supplying additional information."

For me, sunshine "sheds light on" my still life compositions, making them come alive with colors and reflections. Often, as I did here, I will set simple objects by a window and wait for the sun to enter, bringing its magic. When the afternoon sun sheds light in my kitchen, the room comes alive with sunlight filtering through the trees, then dappling across everything within its reach.

I'm captivated by the transformation that occurs as I watch a dull room come to life—a glistening place of welcomed joy, comfort, warmth, and delight. Objects on my table are altered from their common shapes into treasures of beauty. In this painting, the white pitcher reflects the surrounding yellows and violets, the apples shine, revealing new dimensions, and even the dull wooden bowl is further warmed with an orange glow. I've used artificial light in my studio for the same purpose, but it never seems to provide the inspiration I need in order to create.

The kitchen is my favorite room of my house. It is the heart and soul of our home—a place to experience light being shed in various ways. When we invite family, friends, neighbors, and sometimes strangers into our home for a meal, it's more than sharing food; it's the sharing of each other's lives. We may want to bless people with our food, but they, in turn, bless us with the insights they bring into the conversations shared. This, too, is "light" that gives a new perspective, new ideas, and fresh wisdom that illuminates both our minds and hearts.

After the sun has danced for a few hours, it slowly makes its exit through the western windows, signaling the end of the day. You can't see the sunset from here, but you do see the effect the sun has on the tree branches as they play their game of hide-and-seek. And you see glimpses of pinks and oranges as the sun dips down below the horizon, still radiating color throughout the sky and clouds.

During the late fall and winter, when the sun sets earlier, we light candles for the dinner hour. The shedding of this candlelight gives an entirely different emotional "light." Turning off the harsh ceiling flood lamps, and lighting a candle on my kitchen table, transforms the room into an intimate place to talk as JD and I dine together, just the two of us these days.

The candlelight casts warm shadows on our faces, rendering softer gazes. Candlelight sheds a mutual understanding of our hearts and minds, quieting our sometimes anxious emotions, giving rise to peaceful insight. The mess (and I do create a mess when I cook) in the kitchen fades from sight, so our focus is only on our meal and each other. Candlelight brings a different clarity and reflection to this small space as we eat, illuminating what seems essential in our lives: the God that provides us with all good things, the relationships close at hand, and the food that's before us, resulting in harmonious thankfulness.

I need light to see. I need others' light to gain wisdom and understanding. I need light to feel the warmth. I need God's light to bring transparency to my soul and to shed my light. His light is clarifying, insightful, and spiritual. It exposes me for who I am and brings hope to who I want to become. His light will provide understanding and wisdom as I live in the future.

This painting represents my need for light in my life on so many different levels. When the light of the sun shines on this white pitcher, it takes on the colors of silver, gold, purples, and blues. The apples come alive, begging to be eaten. You don't see the sun; you only see the results of the sun. Just so, I can't see God, but I can see the result of God's light in my life, and I hope to be able to reflect the colors of His light and love to others.

"Oh, God, please shine on me!"

———

"God is light; in him is no darkness at all. If we walk in the light as he
is in the light we have fellowship with one another . . ."
(1 John 1:5b, 7, NIV)

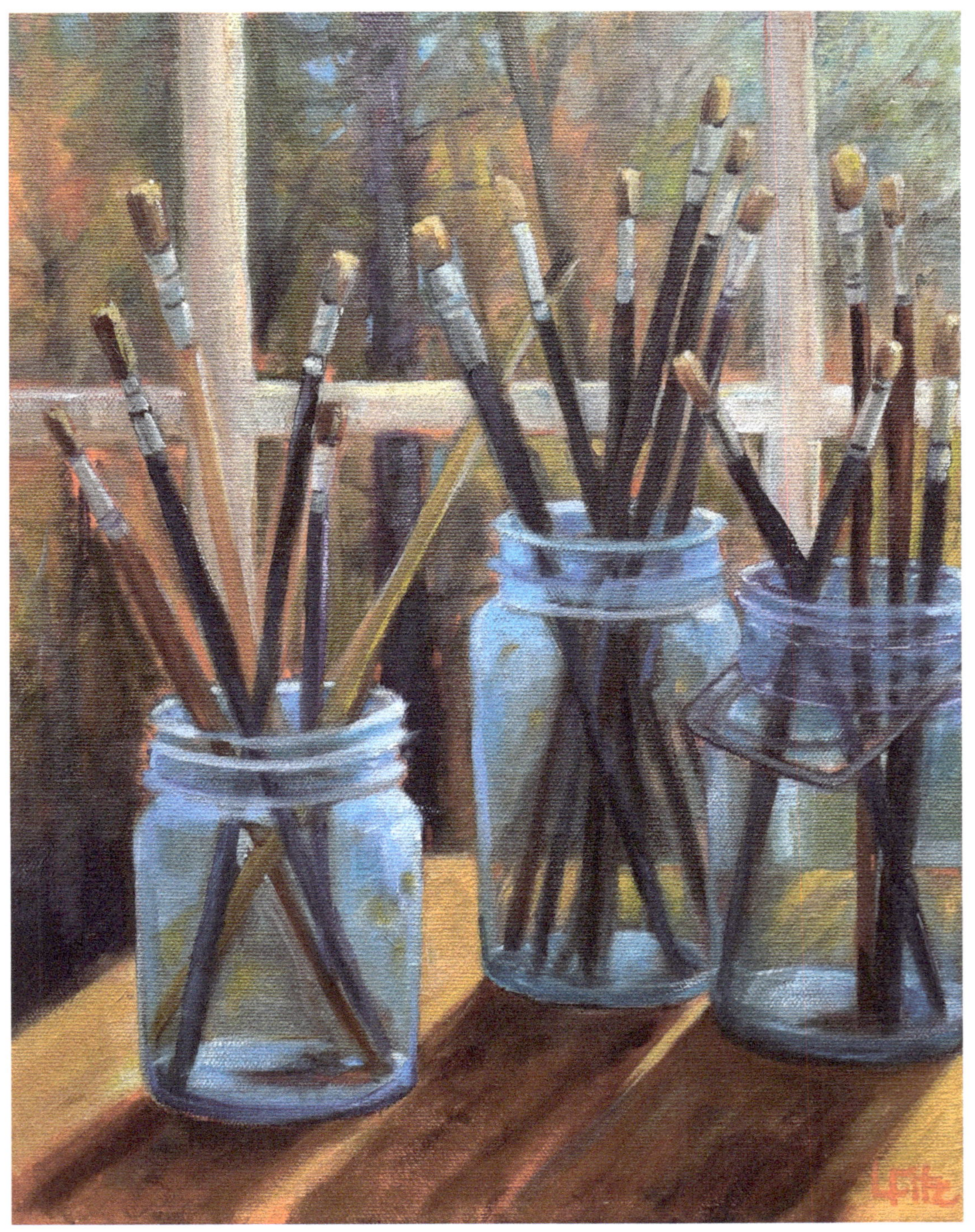

OIL PAINTING, *READY WHEN YOU ARE!* © 2019 LEIGH D. FITZ; WRITING, 2012

No Doubt about It

Past doubts have kept me from my paintbrushes or my pen. That's because doubt, in a matter of minutes, can slip silently into the back door of my mind and hold me captive for days until all hope is drained, leaving me paralyzed on the cold kitchen floor of indecision.

Doubt is a word that, when invited in, gets many people, like me, into trouble. Uncertainty can lead quickly to despair.

"I doubt that."

"I have my doubts."

"I doubt I can do it."

"I doubt that will happen."

"I doubt I could."

"I doubt I'll get well."

"I doubt he loves me."

"I doubt I can achieve that dream."

"I doubt it."

"I doubt . . . "

Doubt brings us to a standstill, stops production, damages dreams, strips us of our hopes, and keeps ideas locked away. Doubts can be life-changing if taken too seriously. Doubt can question our abilities, our God, and those we love. Uncertainty restrains us from our full potential, achieving our goals, or living our dreams. Doubt can make us suspicious, cynical, and harbor a lack of trust.

Doubts also keep us from imagining what could be, holding us back from relationships, job opportunities, adventure, or education. Doubts keep us stagnant. Uncertainty can create loneliness and isolation.

Doubt destroys.

If I hover behind the fear of failure or an obstacle of doubt that I perceive is too great to move beyond, progress stops abruptly, and I use that doubt as an excuse to remain where I am. If I stay where I am in life, my brain and emotions can become rigid or paralyzed, which leads to a weakened state of frailty. With this attitude, no success can emerge. I remain frozen, unable to act on my purpose, my intentions, my dreams. My brushes stay in their jars and my words hidden in journals.

I've wanted to create this book for over ten years. My brushes have been neatly arranged, I've had ample supply of paint and time, and many pages have already been written, and paintings long done. I have support from my husband, and desire in my heart . . . but doubt stands boldly before me, declaring me unfit for such a task: *NOT GOOD ENOUGH!* it shouts, and I listen.

Jesus' disciple, Thomas, doubted that his Master had risen from the dead and wanted to see proof before he believed. When the disciples told him, "We have seen the Lord!" Thomas said of Jesus, "I won't believe it unless I see the nail wounds in his hands, put my fingers into them, and place my hand into the wound in his side."[9] Thomas had his doubts, and he decided to keep them unless he received proof and saw Jesus for himself.

Jesus appeared before His disciples a week later in a locked room. He greeted them all and said, "Peace be with you." Then he looked to Thomas, saying, "Put your finger here, and look at my hands. Put your hand into the wound in my side. Don't be faithless any longer. Believe!"

Thomas cried out, "My Lord and my God!"

Jesus replied, "You believe because you have seen me. Blessed are those who believe without seeing me."[10]

Thomas eventually believed, but certainly missed a blessing because of his doubt. It makes me wonder, *What doubts hold me hostage until I see proof? Do I need proof to determine whether I believe? Do doubts keep me from moving forward with my goals? Does uncertainty keep me from being in a trusting, loving relationship with my spouse? Does doubt keep me from fulfilling my dreams? Does doubt keep me from fully believing my God?*

I guess I've concluded that doubt isn't instigated by God. He says believe in Him without seeing, without proof, and you will be blessed. It takes faith to believe.

I ~~doubt~~ believe it!

I ~~doubt~~ believe I can!

I ~~doubt~~ believe!

What a difference a single word can make in the way a day turns out, the way a year turns out, the way life turns out. Belief versus doubt. God says to stop doubting and believe. I'm not keeping company with doubt. I'm choosing to believe.

I can't see what the future holds, but I want to live into my future without suspicion holding me back from believing in the possibilities or the wonderment of what could be. I have a firm belief in my God whether or not I see proof. I believe, no doubt about it!

9. John 20:24, NLT
10. John 20:29, NLT

"The secret to abundant life: to believe that God is where you doubt He can be."

Ann Voskamp , *The Greatest Gift*

Then Jesus told him, "You believe because you have seen me.
Blessed are those who believe without seeing me."

(John 20:29, NIV)

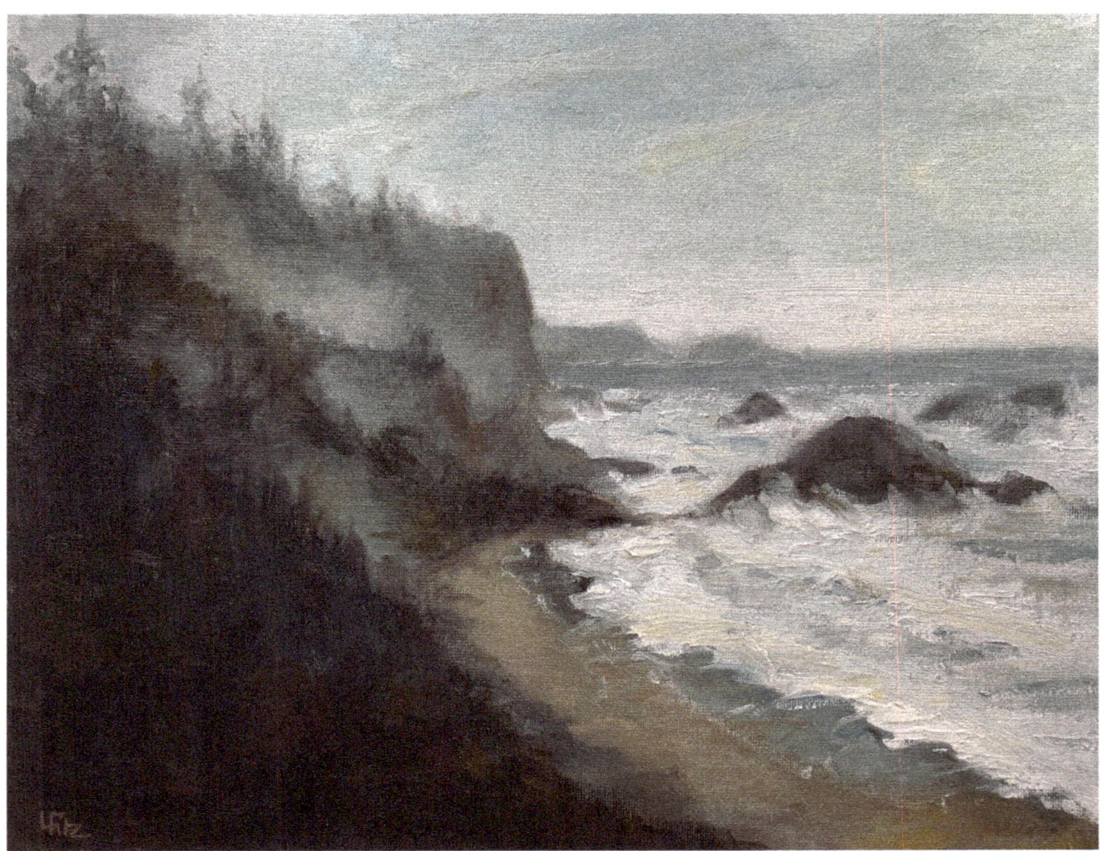

OIL PAINTING, *CHAOTIC BEAUTY* © 2019 LEIGH D. FITZ; WRITING, 2019

Chaotic Beauty

Standing on this cliff alone, trying to still my anxious thoughts, felt like a tumultuous task. I was taking a plein air workshop (painting in outdoor light and air) on the Oregon coast, and I thought if I arrived early to our workshop meeting place, I could calm myself and focus on what I wanted to paint. But, honestly, my real motive was to get a head start before the rest of the class arrived. I needed to think without the pressures of others watching me.

I drew thumbnail sketches, found just the right spot to set up my easel, and started mixing paint. As I watched my classmates arrive, confidently doing the same, I felt they were all considerately more accomplished artists than I was. The voice of self-doubt whispered in my ear that I wasn't as skilled. Over the first two days of the course, I kept comparing my work to theirs and felt mine was sorely lacking.

On the third day, the weather was beautiful, but chaotic and daunting—it matched the thoughts crowding my mind. Fog mingled amongst the cliffs, obscuring the lines, softening the edges. The sun would alter all of it in a couple of hours, not giving me ample time to capture the emotion or the landscape of that early morning moment. I felt hurried, but my brush was frozen on the canvas—how could I paint the power of the sea, the sound of the waves dashing the rocks, the chill in the morning air, or the wild beat of my heart?

I initially lingered with my doubts, allowing them to pick at my scab of insecurity—which left me feeling worse than before. I wanted to prove the value of my work and feel the appreciation and respect of the instructor and other students. Then I realized that the source of my stiffness wasn't just fear or anxiety, it was pride. I knew what I had to do—pride never looks good on the canvas! I attempted to relax my unsettled mind amidst the chaos of the crashing waves, but it proved unnerving, so I decided to lean into the emotion which the scene instilled in me, "chaotic beauty."

Even when the sun came out, lifting the fog, causing the ocean to sparkle with joy, I was determined to discipline myself, stay with my original emotion, and not be swayed. In the end, very little paint or time went into the actual painting, because my brush got on board and moved with the quickened pace of the weather change.

Nature never pauses, even as I hurry to catch up. Most of the time creation calms me, and makes me want to take a deep breath and consider the magnitude of God's handiwork. This time, however, I knew I had to scramble to capture His work and my emotions as they were in that moment, before they faded away. I couldn't wait for a tranquil mind to show up. As uncomfortable as it was, I had to embrace the chaos.

At the end of that day, the painting felt honest. I liked the unfinished feel. When I got home, I thought I would add more paint, but I didn't dare touch it, for fear I might paint over that emotional moment and lose the essence of the chaotic beauty I had captured.

Impressionism is a way to express artistically what you see and receive in the moment—impressionist paintings are just that—impressions. This painting and writing are my impressions, not to be feared or repaired or judged. The moment I silence my pen or hush my paintbrush out of fear of being judged too harshly by my audience, I slip away into a mute existence of loneliness. I am learning that to fail miserably as an artist (or as a person) is better than to never attempt to create—or live—at all.

The voice of the Lord is over the waters; the God of glory thunders,
and the Lord, over many waters; the voice of the Lord is powerful;
the voice of the Lord is full of majesty."
(Psalm 29:3-4, ESV)

God's Tender Love

I grew up believing that God loves the whole world. I knew this included me, but I assumed that since He loved everyone, His love was a generic sort of love. It seemed impossible to grasp the concept that He loved me personally. I was certain I wasn't lovable or deserving of His love. I imagined He was always disappointed with me for various reasons and when I messed up (which was often), He walked away. That changed.

I was thirty-two when my doctor told me that endometriosis had spread extensively to my ovaries and bowel and it was essential I have a total hysterectomy. He scheduled my surgery for a week or so later. When I got home from my doctor's visit, I threw myself on my bed and cried over this impending loss of my reproductive system and any female hormones, which would thrust me into early menopause. I begged God to heal me, to spare me from this surgery. I felt too young to lose this part of myself and I didn't think I knew anyone my age who had gone through this. I had no one to speak with about my concerns and questions. I felt alone. I cried out to God to help me. And then the phone rang.

To my shock, it was my sister calling from Kenya! In those days, it was an expensive proposition to make a call to the States. She lived in a remote area and therefore we rarely talked, even though we were very close in spirit. When I heard her voice, I remembered her unbelievable loss a few years earlier when her third baby, James, died in the last month of her pregnancy due to complications that were life threatening to her as well. She was flown to Nairobi for the delivery, followed by an emergency hysterectomy in order to save her life. Tragically, this also meant the loss of future children.

I told her of my impending surgery and, no surprise, she knew what I was going through and what I needed to hear. I don't remember the exact words, but I do remember silently weeping as she ministered words of grief over my loss with a tenderness of love mingled with hope. I was stunned by the timing of the phone call.

Two weeks later, I was checked into the hospital the night before surgery to do prep work, to ready my system for the complicated surgery that would keep me there for a week while I recovered. It was during this prep work that my nurse asked if she could bring me my slippers. I told her I hadn't brought slippers. She chided me for the lack of planning and told me to call my husband to bring them in the morning, to which I replied, "I don't own a pair of slippers."

That night as I lay in my hospital bed, I kept thinking about why it was that I hadn't remembered to buy myself a pair of slippers. Now it was too late! How would my husband even have the time to go looking for slippers? How would I describe to him the right pair that I wanted—something cozy, maybe leather with fur lining? And would slippers even be available this time of year in the stores? (This was before Uggs or the internet were invented.) I further berated myself for worrying over slippers when I should be praying about surgery and asking God to help me feel at peace, but all I could think about was slippers.

The next morning, my husband arrived with a box wrapped in brown paper with foreign stamps and a return address from Kenya. In 1984, it took months to send anything through the mail. But my sister had sent me a box! I tore the paper away and opened it. In the box I found God's love for me personally—in the form of slippers. I wept with joy. To me it was as if God Himself had tenderly, lovingly placed a pair of slippers in my hands to remind me that His love for me was not generic but extremely personal, right down to details of being fur-lined leather in exactly my size! At just the right moment, in just the right place, God provided just the right pair of slippers for me! A miracle! The unimaginable had occurred—God loved me!

Knowing that you're thoroughly loved is a game changer. I felt valued by God. My belief in God deepened. I continued (and still continue) to go through the disciplines of belief. But the "shoulds" and the "oughts" are diminished by my desire to love God. Desire overtook duty as my motivation and now I get to love and serve this amazing God, not because I "should," but because I want to.

*"Let the beloved of the Lord rest secure in him for He shields him all day long
and the one whom the Lord loves rests between his shoulders."*
(Deuteronomy 33:12, NIV)

*"I pray that out of his glorious riches he may strengthen you with power through his Spirit
in your inner being so that Christ may dwell in your hearts through faith. And I pray that
you, being rooted and established in love, may have the power, together with all the Lord's
holy people, to grasp how wide and how long and how high and deep is the love of Christ and
to know his love that surpasses knowledge—that you may be filled to the measure of all the
fullness of God."*
(Ephesians 3:16–19, NIV)

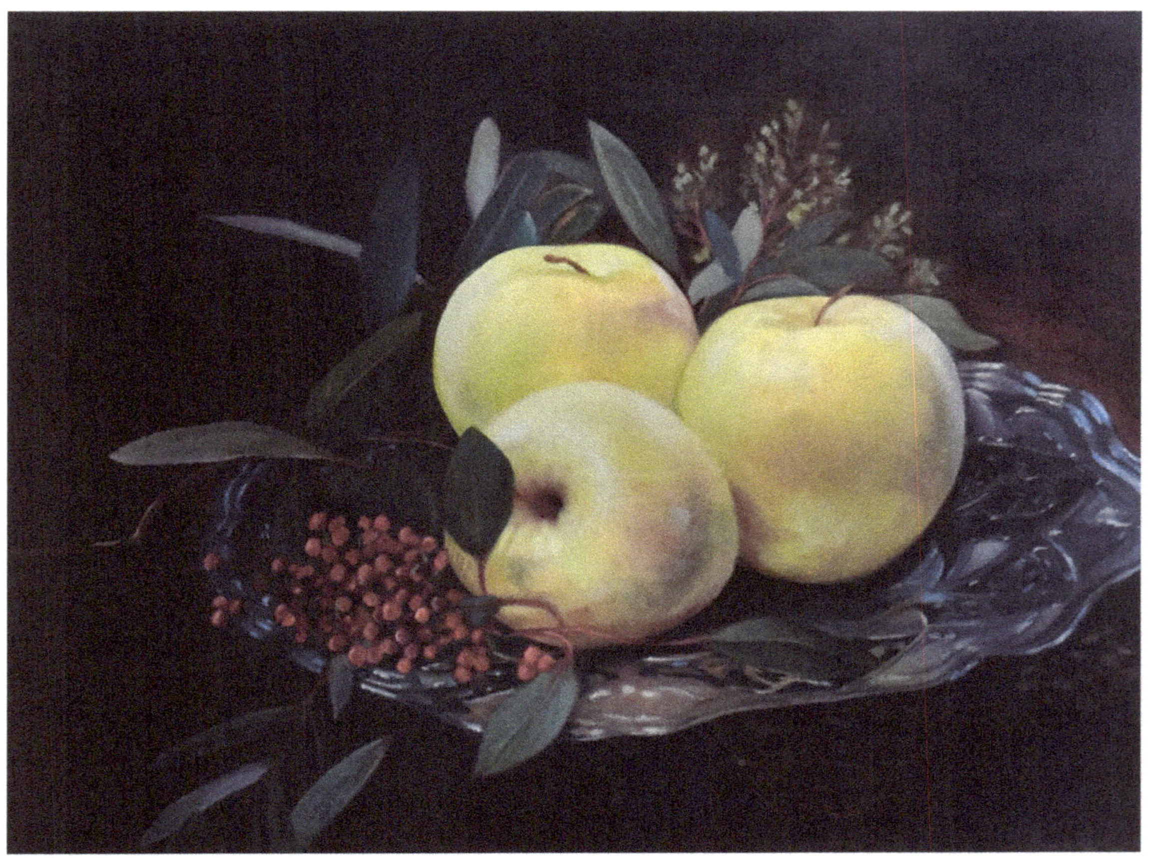

OIL PAINTING, *A NOURISHING WORD* © 2011 LEIGH D. FITZ

Words Aptly Spoken

As I was cutting golden apples for my Thanksgiving stuffing, I recalled the verse in Proverbs that states, "A word aptly spoken is like apples of gold in settings of silver." The beginnings of an idea for a painting started to form in my mind's eye, so I quickly stopped to exchange my knife for my camera and went searching for the silver plate my great aunt had given me. Capturing the idea in pictures would provide a reference for a future painting.

Words. This painting is of apples, but it's really about the power of words. Words can either feed the heart or slice a soul. Words have the power to instruct or damage, to build up or to tear down, to nourish or starve an individual. Words that were given to me in childhood, like "stupid," are not easily erased and still, today, have the power to strip my confidence to shreds. Maybe this is one of the reasons I want to choose my words wisely. There is an abundance of them available, but sometimes I'm not always willing to take the time to give them thoughtfully. At times, I hand them out recklessly before thinking. This was the main reason I had committed the above verse to memory, but, apparently, memorizing a proverb is not equivalent to abiding by it.

Lovingly chosen words, at just the right moment, can make all the difference in giving a beautiful gift to a lonely person, a lifesaver to an insecure child, reassurance to a discouraged spouse, or peace to an anxious friend. I want to be intentional to give words to others that are tasty and sustaining (like apples), and that will be treasured (like silver).

Unfortunately, words can't be retrieved once they're out of my mouth, but I can ask for forgiveness, giving them kind words to replace the harsh. (I'm speaking from experience on this one!)

This painting now hangs in my dining room—a room designed for eating and conversation. At a glance, it is a reminder to me to choose carefully the words I give, and to be thankful for the choice words I've been given over the years that were like golden apples, served to nourish my soul.

"Wise words satisfy like a good meal; the right words bring satisfaction.
The tongue can bring death or life . . ."
(Proverbs 18:20-21a, NLT)

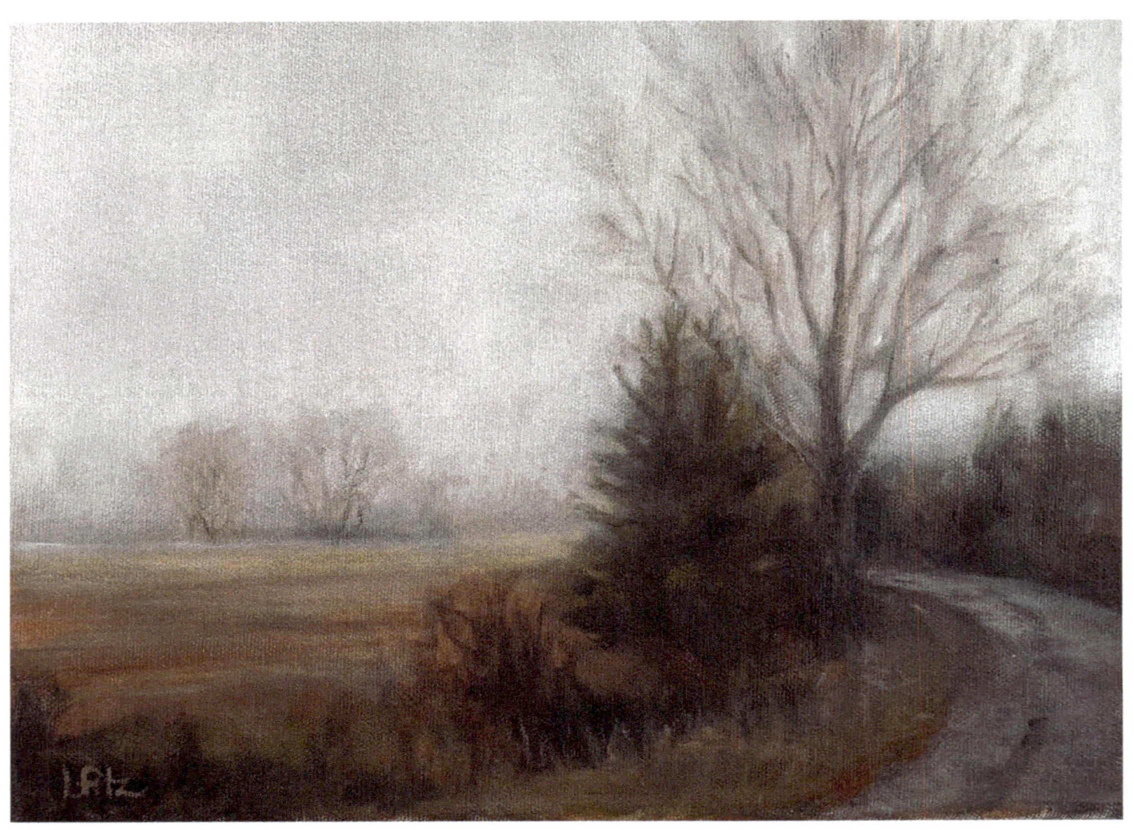

OIL PAINTING, *FEELING FALLOW* ©2021 LEIGH D. FITZ

Winters

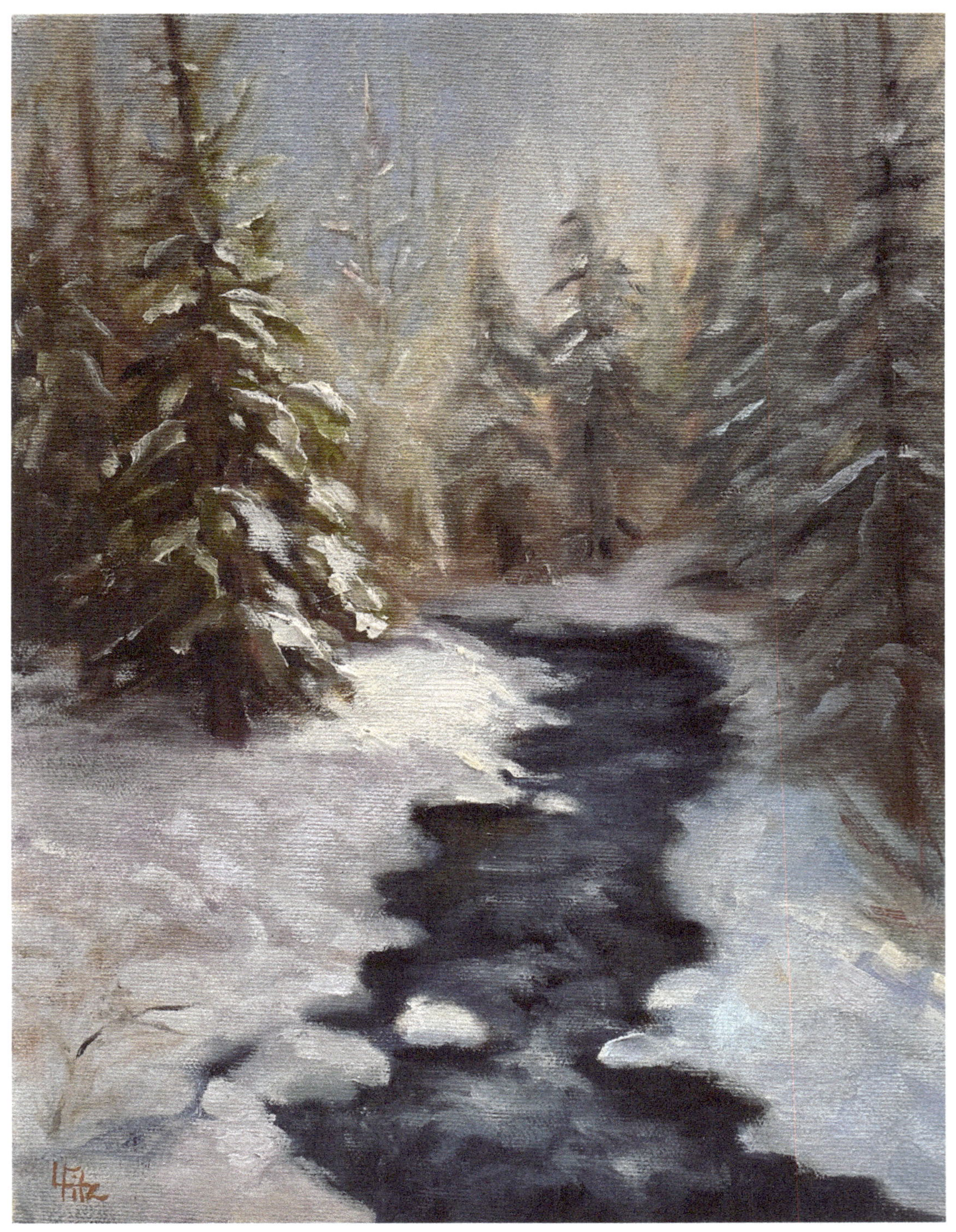

OIL PAINTING, *WONDERMENT* © 2013 LEIGH D. FITZ

Am I Ready for Christmas?

As I sit with my tea in the morning light, I begin my internal conversation, my musings. *Do I really want Christmas to come?* To be honest, in this stage of my life, I sometimes answer myself, *No, not really.*

Christmas has changed so much for me that I can hardly find it anymore under the disguise of its worldly wrappings. I don't recognize it. Oh, I know the name, but my love for it has diminished as I focus on the details that have to get done. The meaning seems to have been lost, much like a once well-loved teddy bear that has lost its stuffing. I loved it once but now have moved on to something new. I still celebrate the "holidays," but do I still know and celebrate Christmas?

I look for it as I unpack decorations and lights. I think, *Surely I will experience it as I buy presents for others,* but then find myself eyeing gifts I want instead. I may even go to church an extra time or two around the holidays because isn't that the right thing to do? Invariably, it will give me a warm fuzzy feeling, right? And maybe that's why I don't want it to come this year. It feels phony. I don't want to go through the motions of Christmas without recognizing the meaning.

I wonder what the "Birthday Boy" would ask me for? Lights, trees, packages wrapped and given to others instead of him? Perhaps, but I think He would appreciate if I were more contemplative as I approach the day. Yet there is much to accomplish and so many items to check off lists. I try to do all of this for others, but maybe I'm missing the real joy, not the mustered-up excitement I generate around my grandchildren. Am I keeping them from seeing Christmas—the real Christmas—by my "mustering"?

I can't remember a Christmas where, from the moment I awoke I wished Jesus "Happy Birthday" from deep within me. A Christmas where I have offered gifts, made a cake, or written a card or note of love to Him. Have I ever just hung out with Him all day, attempting to make it the "best birthday ever," like I did for my kids long ago?

Oh Jesus, come to me this year fresh and new and not bound by the rules of Christmas. You came two thousand years ago to give us Yourself as a gift. The greatest gift. And just like You always do, You keep giving gifts all year long, even on Your own birthday.

How do you want me to get ready for Christmas? What do you really want for your birthday? Just let me know, I have Amazon Prime!

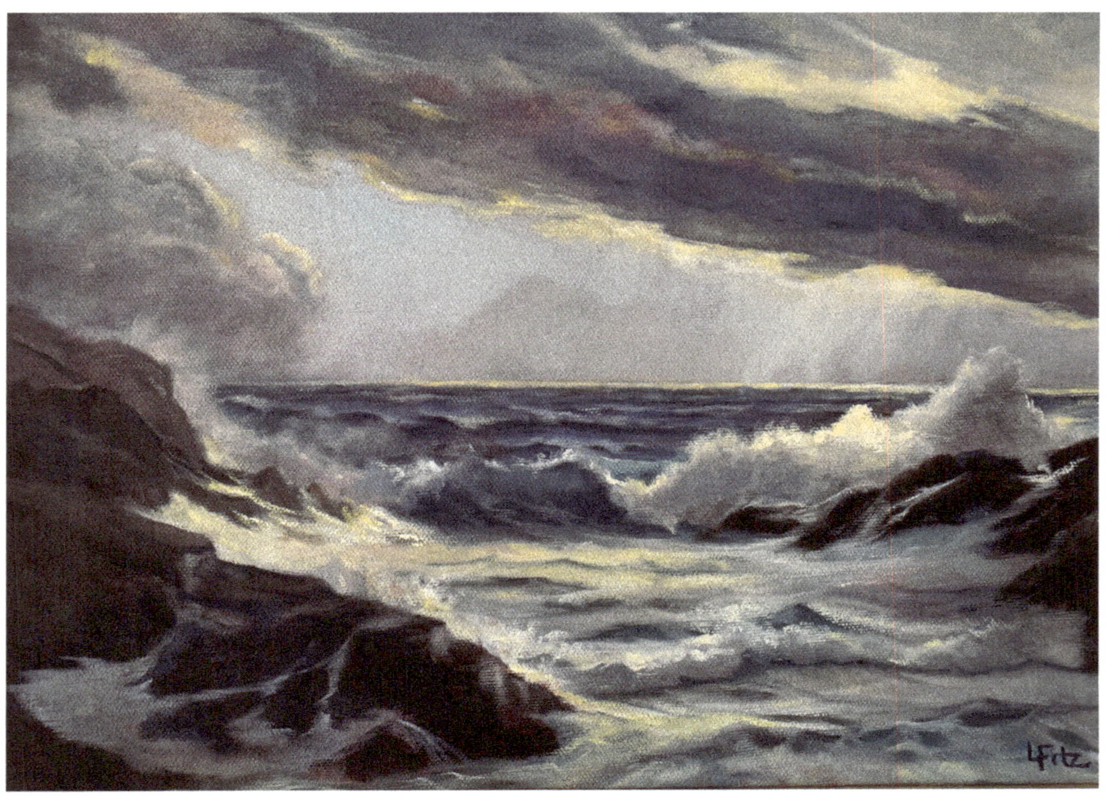

OIL PAINTING, *EVEN THE WIND AND THE WAVES OBEY* © 2018 LEIGH D. FITZ; WRITING, 2018

Even the Wind and Waves Obey Him

Be Still My Soul

Be still, my soul; the Lord is on thy side;

Bear patiently the cross of grief or pain;

Leave to thy God to order and provide;

In every change He faithful will remain.

Be still, my soul; thy best, thy heavenly, Friend

Through thorny ways leads to a joyful end.

Be still, my soul; thy God doth undertake

To guide the future as He has the past.

Thy hope, thy confidence, let nothing shake;

All now mysterious shall be bright at last.

Be still, my soul; the waves and winds still know

His voice who ruled them while He dwelt below.

~ Katharine Von Schlegal

Early in January of 2018, I was informed of a mass present on my mammogram that required a biopsy right away, and which would eventually lead to my cancer diagnosis. It was a Tuesday morning and they wanted to schedule the biopsy for the following Friday, but JD and I were planning on going to the coast for a week and I didn't want to miss it. So, I scheduled the biopsy for the following week and left town. I wasn't worried because I had undergone a biopsy before and it had been benign. I didn't want to ruin a perfectly great trip.

I think God in His wisdom was preparing me for the inevitable. One of the days we were on the Pacific Coast, there was a storm surge that brought the tide in much higher than usual. I watched it from the window. It was a visual reminder of the power of the ocean and how the water cannot be controlled or held back. I also remembered how the disciples were overwhelmed by the power Jesus displayed as He spoke to the storm and hushed it with just a few words. They marveled, "Even the wind and the waves obey him."

JD and I talked about the "what ifs," and prayed for the strength we would need if we received an answer we didn't want. I started this painting as I waited for the biopsy results that would ultimately have the word "cancer" in print. I desperately needed a visual reminder that the God who created and controlled the winds and the waves was able to hold me securely through this next storm of life.

I treasure a quote by Nicky Gumbel, an English Anglican priest and author. He wrote, "Sometimes Jesus calms the storm. Sometimes he lets the storm rage and He calms you." The latter was my experience. Cancer, like a hurricane, can turn deadly and leave disaster in its wake. I knew the potential havoc this could cause on my life. At times I couldn't keep my head above water, but God provided others to buoy me and keep me from drowning.

As I was painting this seascape, I wondered if the storm was just brewing or finally passing me by. When my mind drifted to worry, God brought gentle reminders that He was holding me close and keeping me afloat, filling me with peace. In my weakened state, I felt too weary to pray, but that was okay, too, for God in His mercy didn't require anything of me.

In the months following my diagnosis, He provided family and friends to care, encourage, and pray for me. It's humbling to receive help. But even though the storm felt like it would never end, God provided calm in my mind. He held on to me, whispering reassurance that He was present, and that He had power—even over cancer. Painting this seascape was a helpful reminder to me to keep trusting God through the inevitable "storms" of life, especially when I don't get the diagnoses I hope for.

You faithfully answer our prayers with awesome deeds,

O God our savior.

You are the hope of everyone on earth,

even those who sail on distant seas.

You formed the mountains by Your power

and armed yourself with mighty strength.

You quieted the raging oceans

with their pounding waves

and silenced the shouting of the nations.

Those who live at the ends of the earth

stand in awe of Your wonders.

From where the sun rises to where it sets,

You inspire shouts of joy.

(Psalm 65:5-8, NLT)

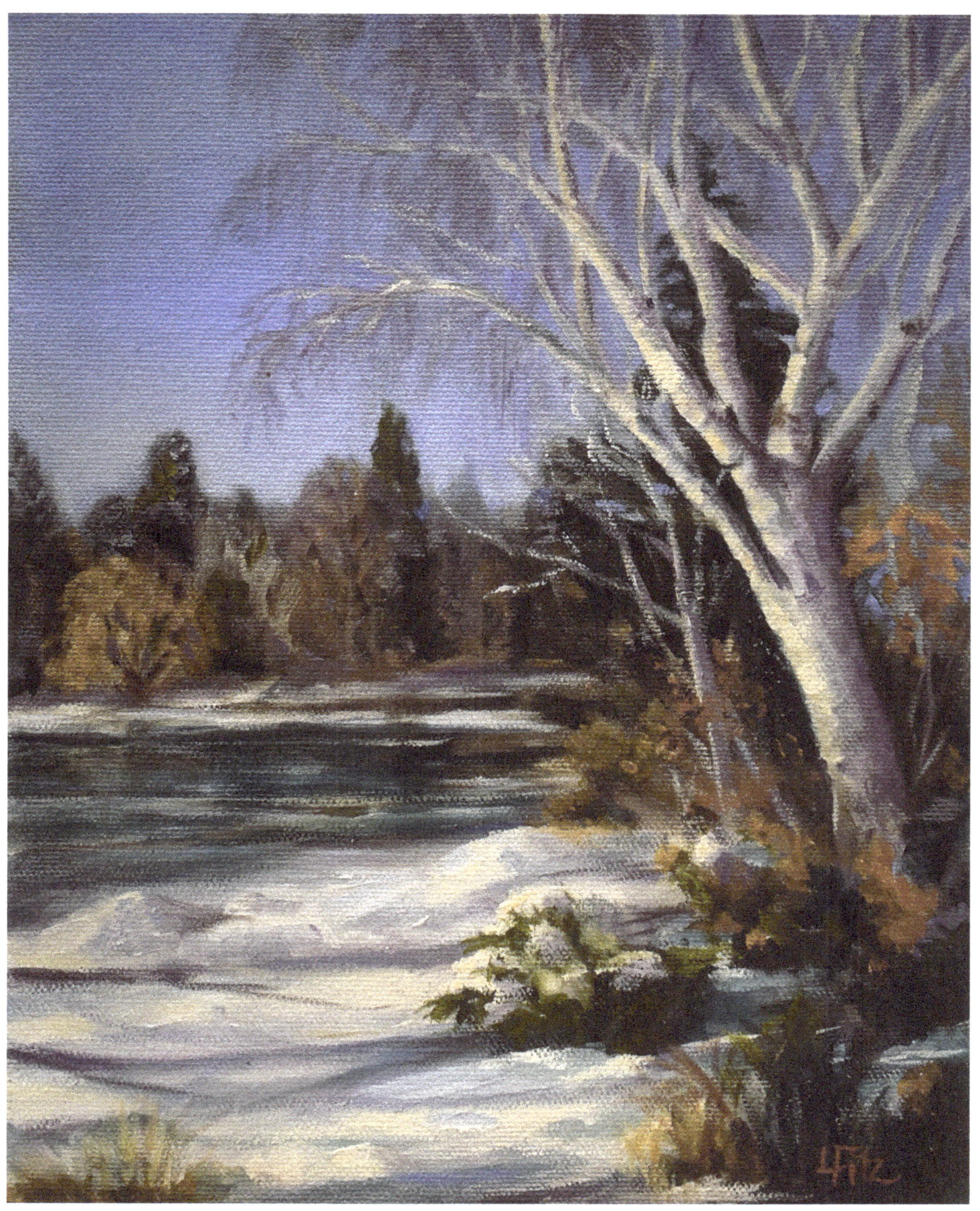

OIL PAINTING, *DRESSED FOR SUCCESS* © LEIGH D. FITZ; WRITING, 2011

Don't Miss the Memory

The transforming power of a snowfall always leaves me transfixed at my window. It's as if God has dressed up His creation in its finest! Even decrepit buildings, cluttered yards, and misshapen trees look beautiful clothed in pure white on a winter morning..

Waking up to a new snowfall is one of my favorite memories from childhood. It meant perhaps school would be closed (always a good idea in my mind) and I could play to my heart's content, making forts, snowmen, and having snowball battles with the neighbor kids. I remember a night on which my dad took us tobogganing. He lined us up according to size, and, being the littlest, I was in the very front. That set me up to see firsthand just how fast we plunged down the hill. It was terrifying and glorious all in the same moment.

Yesterday, I woke to freshly fallen snow. I sat all cozy and warm with tea in hand, watching the "show" outside my window. (Have you ever noticed how snow silences the world? It is stillness like no other.) I sat, once again, amazed by the creativity of God.

Then the doorbell rang. *Who would come calling at this hour?* I wondered. I opened the door to see my two adorable grandchildren waiting outside, followed by my daughter, who asked if I had an extra pair of mittens for her. "Sure," I said happily as I closed the door behind me to keep the cold out. I found mittens and was about to head back to the door to give them to her when I realized I was letting the opportunity for a great memory to slip away in exchange for a chair and a cup of tea. I remembered that I have to be careful of which doors I close. So, I dressed quickly, pulled on my boots, and with two sets of mittens in hand, I headed for the door with the excitement of a young girl eager to go sledding.

We laughed, made snow angels, and pretended that my daughter and I were horses pulling a sleigh (neighs and all) while singing, "Over the river and through the woods to grandmother's house we go, the horse knows the way to carry the sleigh . . ." (You get the idea.) We went sledding down a pristine snow-covered hill and screamed with delight as we bailed out at the end of the ride so we wouldn't hit the fence at the bottom. At one point, I grabbed the sled from my grandson to show him how to get a running start—jumping on face first for a super-fast ride down the hill (and enduring some very sore muscles the next day).

Then, as fast as it had begun, the magic was over. My grandkids were cold, and it was time to go home. But as I walked down my street, laughing to myself, I was flooded with gratefulness that I had not just handed over the mittens, but instead had put a pair on myself as well and joined them—making a memory.

Just as I recall memories of sledding growing up, I hope my daughter and grandkids remember the day I played with them in the snow! Life moves fast . . . don't miss it!

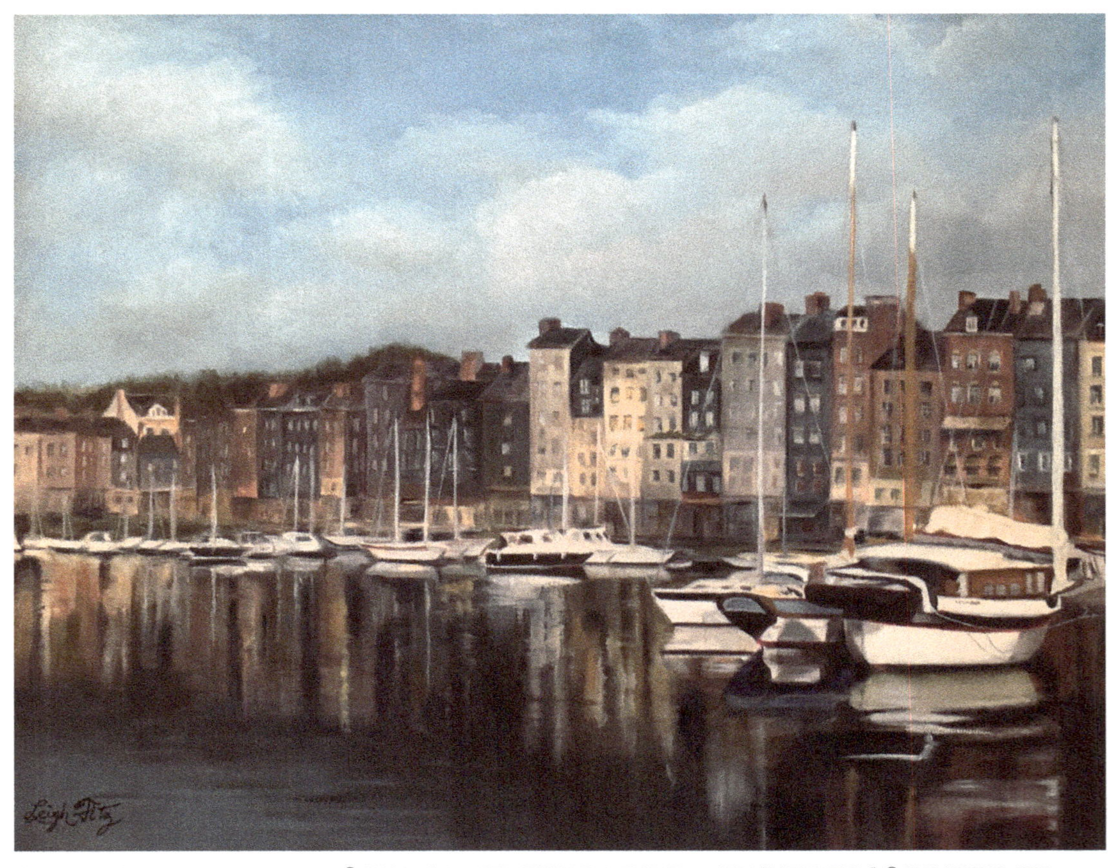

OIL PAINTING, *TUCKED IN FOR THE NIGHT* © 2002 LEIGH D. FITZ (HONFLEUR, FRANCE); POEM, "SAFE WITHIN" © 2019 LEIGH D. FITZ

Safe Within

Lost in a sea of stress
Sinking beneath waves of worry
Direction lost in darkest night.
My cries heard, despite thunder
The storm of "what ifs" calmed
The winds of doubt, hushed
My fears rescued
Safe within.

Turning my eyes
To thank my rescuer
For pulling me out of the depth
Suddenly finding in its place
Quiet dawn as it awakes
And reaching for His embrace
Finding I'm already there
Safe within.

Safe within
No storm can break
Held secure from wind or wake
No danger lurks
No risk of harm
Gentle swaying brings a calm
Lulls to sleep in loving arms
Safe within.

I like to play it safe. Whenever my kids were leaving the house, the two things I would say were, "I love you," and, "Be careful." And just now, as I'm writing this many years later, I kissed my husband goodbye and said the same thing as he ventured out to go skiing.

I know it's magical thinking to assume that saying, "Be careful," will keep them safe. And I know that whether I say it or not, my family members will undoubtedly be okay. But, again, I like to play it safe, and this is why I'm sitting down safe within my home, writing, instead of skiing down a mountain.

A few years ago, I gave up skiing altogether because it didn't feel safe anymore—the risk simply felt too great for me. I do miss the thrill, the beauty of the snow, and the shared laughter during our time on the slopes. But I don't miss the cold, nor the fear I experienced when I would get going too fast. I certainly don't miss the falls.

However, I can't help but wonder: *If I play it safe all the time, will I miss out on some really great things in life?*

This painting, in a way, describes how I like my life . . . safe within the "harbor." My husband is the risk-taker and would rather be out sailing in harsh winds or water skiing with the saltwater whipping his face and never a care in the world. He would loathe being moored in a harbor of safety! "Boring," he'd say. He doesn't see the danger (and if he does, he doesn't care), and therefore, he embraces life fully. Any experience he desires is his for the taking. (Though he has had his share of accidents and emergency room visits!) I, on the other hand, am not a risk-taker. I see the consequences . . . and I fear failure.

Fear has other ways of permeating my life. I realize I not only let fear bring stress into present situations, but I tend to propel my fear into the future, even when it isn't warranted. Being hearing impaired, I fear going completely deaf; having been treated for breast cancer, I fear that it will return; when I forget words, I fear I'm getting Alzheimer's (like my mother). But I know these situations cannot be altered by playing it safe, no matter what I do.

Being consumed by fear that my safety or security is at risk can potentially paralyze me! Some days, I literally have to hold out my hands to God and ask Him to take this weighty emotion—this burden—away from me. Over time, I have learned I need to actively fix my eyes on God each day, trusting and remembering all that I know about Him. It's in the remembering of His character that I find peace and safety. I don't have to be gripped by fear if I focus on the God who both helps and holds me safe within His keeping.

Each day, I must focus on the fact that my safety rests within Him. As I keep my eyes on Him, He stills my fears, calms the waves, and guides my emotions to a peace that only HE can offer. My always-present protector . . . in my living room or on the slopes.

In God's arms, I find safety. Through His character, I am reminded that He is my safe harbor. Come to think of it, He's keeping my husband there, too.

"Fear not, for I am with you; be not dismayed, for I am your God,
I will strengthen you, I will help you, I will uphold you with my righteous right hand.
For I, the Lord your God, holds your right hand; it is I who says to you,
'Fear not, I am the one who helps you.'"
(Isaiah 42:10,13, ESV)

"He stilled the storm to a whisper; the waves of the sea were hushed.
They were glad when it grew calm, and he guided them to their desired haven."
(Psalm 107:29-30, ESV)

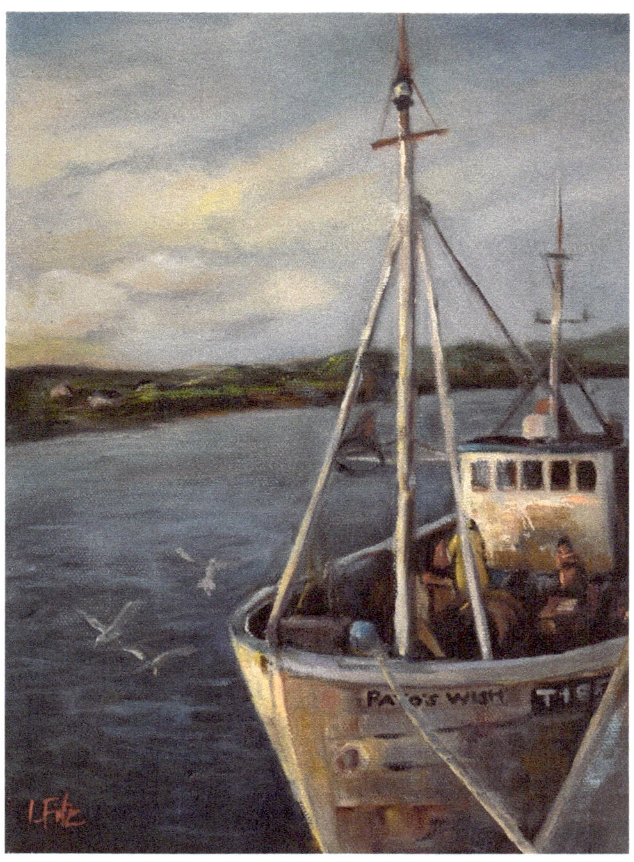

OIL PAINTING, *IRELAND* © LEIGH D. FITZ

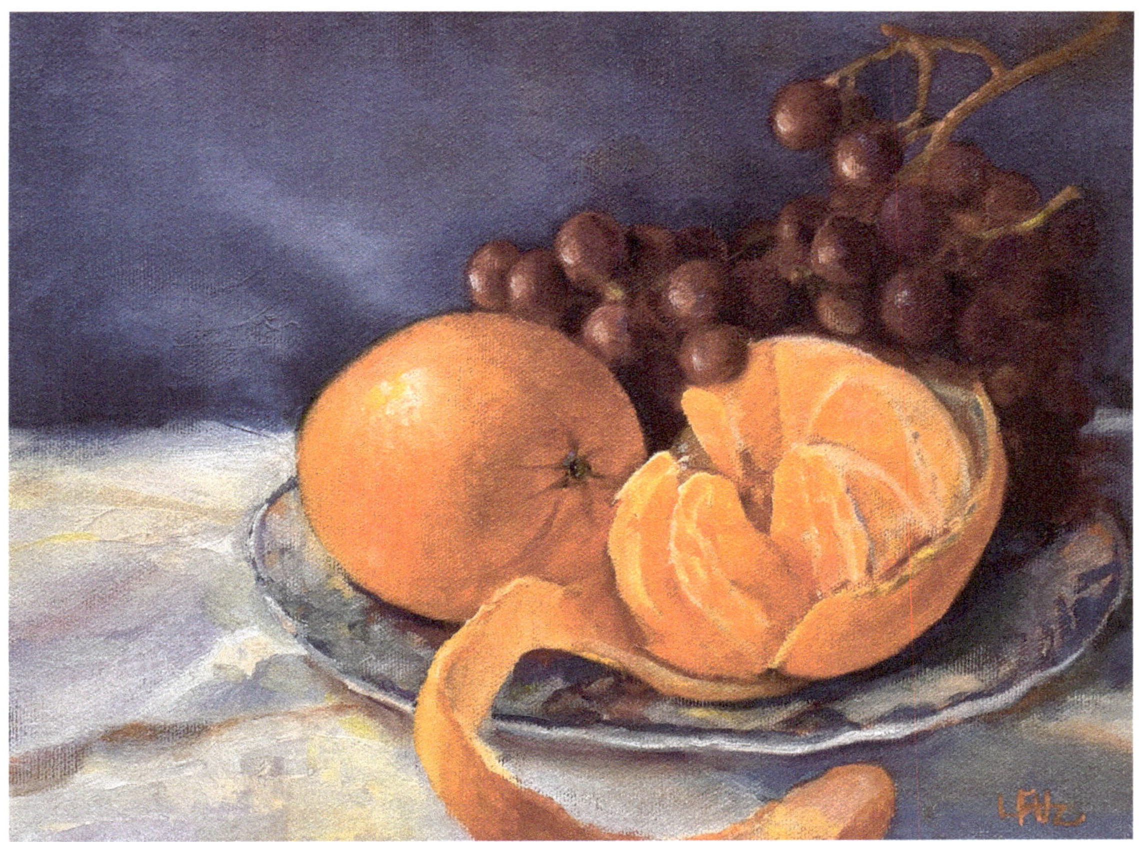

OIL PAINTING, *SHARING AN ORANGE* © 2010 LEIGH D. FITZ; WRITING, 2010

Generosity

This painting began as a study in contrast and complements—the juxtaposition of colors. Orange against its complementary color, blue, opposite on the color wheel.

But while I set up this arrangement, studied the shapes, and began to paint, it prompted me to think about the juxtaposition of two people's inner souls. One, like the orange on the left, is tightly closed, unyielding, greedy with its thoughts and its fruit, unable to share. The other is willing to expose its inner self, generously offering its words and "fruit."

Oranges are so simple to divide, so easily shareable—but once peeled, irreparably opened. Does this happen in real life as well? I believe it does. I ask, "Will there be enough to go around?" Or, "If I share my heart honestly, openly, will I be rejected?" And, "Do generous acts of kindness and sharing of our lives and resources deplete us, or is it the one who withholds who experiences scarcity?"

Within my relationships, I usually have choices—whether to share graciously or hoard my resources. *Am I going to give what I have, or hold tightly to what I possess for myself? Will I peel back my layers to reveal my honest self, or shut my eyes tight, close my mouth, and turn away from the ones I love? Open? Closed? Share? Withhold?*

These questions swirled in my mind as I painted these oranges. I couldn't help thinking about my communications with those closest to me. The peeled orange is an invitation—so full of joy and the desire to share and be tasted—to experience the hidden delight of this fruit. I want to live my life to reflect this spirit but often I hesitate.

A dear friend of mine used to be in the habit of sharing an orange with her husband before bed each night. It turned into a precious memory after he died at the young age of forty. Sharing an orange, sharing words, sharing expressions on our faces, sharing our resources, sharing life, sharing our love as we lean in to hug—all of these are ways to give to one another.

But, in the real world, I've discovered that I don't always feel like sharing my honest self or my resources. Instead, I pull away at times when I should cleave, I turn over in bed and give my back to my husband instead of my kiss goodnight, and I'm sure my silence is loudly heard.

What keeps me from sharing what I have is the notion that there won't be enough. If I genuinely believed that God would provide all my needs (which the Bible promises, P.S.) then I would certainly want to share, wouldn't I? When I don't share, I'm saying, in essence, that I don't trust God for my provision.

Sharing an orange is simple. Sharing my life is complicated. John 15:13 says, "There is no greater love than to lay down one's life for one's friends." This idea is certainly countercultural. This notion of laying down one's life for another person is extreme. Isn't self-protection beneficial to my husband and family? How can I do this and where do I start? I suppose I begin by offering what I have. I begin by sharing my orange.

Post Script:

I wrote this a few years ago at a time when it was easier to share, but now, as I review this in 2020, we are sheltering in place, in the middle of the COVID-19 pandemic. Grocery store shelves are being emptied quickly, and toilet paper, among other things, is difficult to find—I'm sure because of hoarding. Now will be the time when my true colors will be revealed. It's not so easy for me to share when my resources are truly running low.

"Taste and see that the Lord is good;

blessed is the man that takes refuge in him."

(Psalm 34:8, NIV)

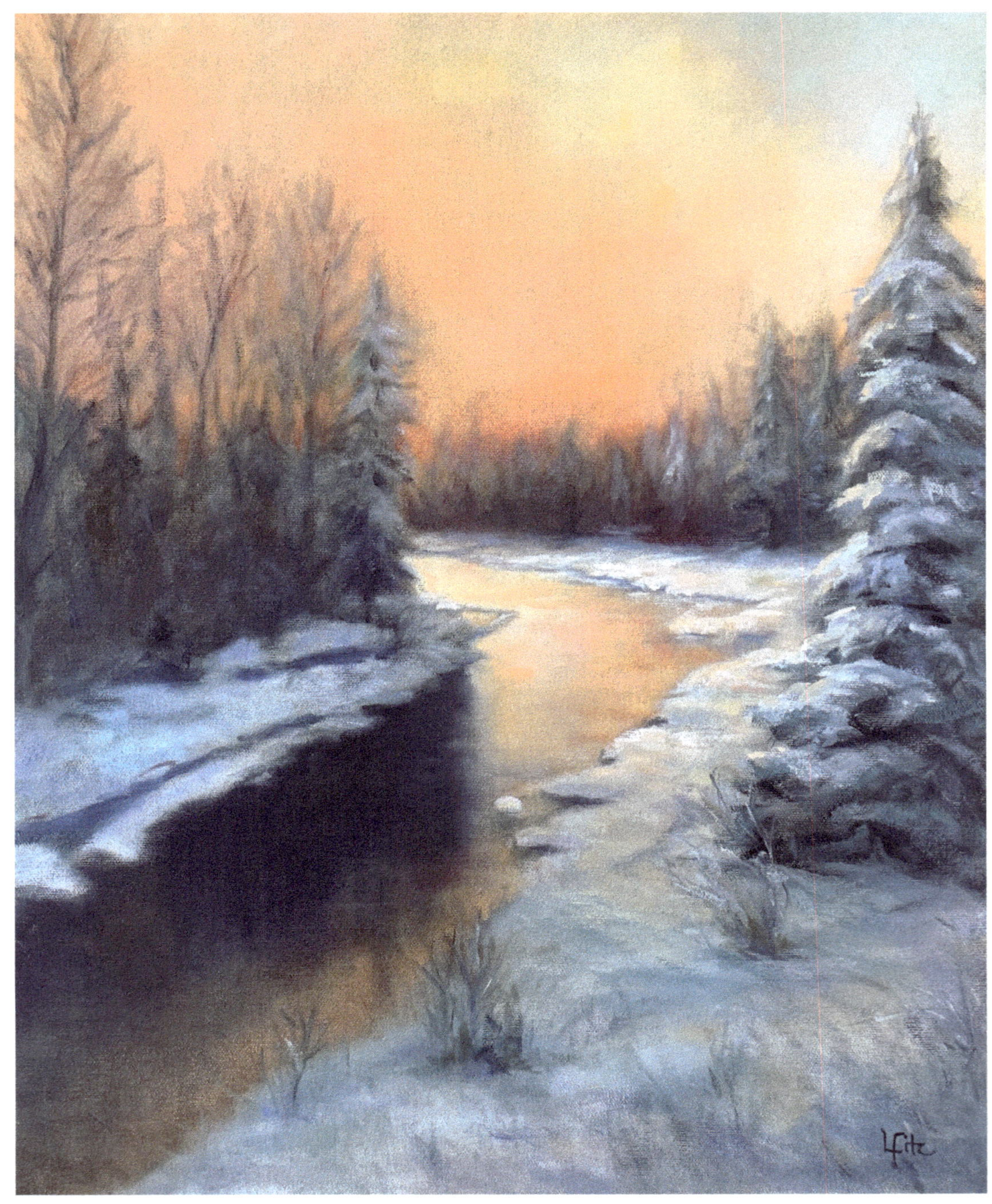

OIL PAINTING, *FINDING THE WARMTH IN WINTER* © 2013 LEIGH D. FITZ; WRITING, 2013

Finding Warmth in Winter

I first painted this winter landscape with a blue sky inspired by a hike alone through fresh fallen snow in Whistler, Canada, yet somehow it didn't match my mood. I was in a dark place and kept asking myself these hard questions: *Knowing there will always be seasons of sadness, loss, pain, and frustration, how do I find warmth in those times? What brings hope?*

When life feels cold and dark, when the light seems to fade, along with my hope, I know I must find warmth to survive. It's difficult for me to trust a God that doesn't always keep me safe, warm, healthy, or free from loss. But who says that out loud? At times like these, I can only ask God to raise my head once more to see His face and feel His warmth.

I have a friend who always seems to be filled with joy, even in the most dire of circumstances. She writes, listing all that she's grateful for, in a journal before bed each night. I, too, started this practice a few years ago after reading Ann Voskamp's book *1000 Gifts*. The key for me is being grateful to God for all the blessings of my life, big and small. It has kept me from the deep, dark pit of self-pity. Focusing on my gains rather than my losses has been a saving grace.

It would be great if life were always fair weather, permanently blessed with the luxury of blue skies, flowers in bloom, and birds singing from the treetops. But here in the Pacific Northwest we have dark, cold, and rainy winters. In my own life, too, winter comes more often than I would like. Days get darker, the nights can seem endlessly long, the soreness of my soul increases, friends can't be found, and God is silent. What then?

I shiver with loneliness, cold from pain, yet Psalm 23 says that He is with me and I lack nothing. God says He restores my soul, but my soul is in disrepair. These verses tell me that He leads me to green pastures, but deep snow is all around me, without a meadow in sight.

The psalmist says He puts food before me and anoints my head with oil. I read the words and my head says I believe, but my heart starts to doubt that God is caring for me personally. I wonder if I've wandered off too far for Him to come and find me? I hear a resounding "NO!" from Heaven at this last thought, for I hold to the promise that I'm never too far from God to be found. And neither are you. I believe He does reach us and comfort us, sometimes in ways we don't see.

I'm not always transparent about my thoughts—to my friends or my family. Sometimes, I pack up my true feelings and those not so pleasant thoughts, and put a false smile on my face as I place my honest self in a box, to be stored until time replaces those thoughts or I forget and move on. But God sees through the phony smile, reads my thoughts, and knows my anxious heart. He's here! I know this, so I'm deciding, just now, to open those boxes of my heart, asking Him to search through them to see what needs to be discarded or kept, cherished or forgotten. Otherwise, I will be loaded down with worries, shame, fear, and the weight of guilt.

So again, I ask you, Lord, to raise my head to see Your face. I need to see Your eyes full of mercy, offered fresh to me in this new morning of life. I need to experience Your love that compels me forward even when I lack energy, or understanding of what I perceive as the dark road I'm traveling.

Even before my whispered prayer has finished falling from my lips, the corners of my mouth begin to turn upward as I sit back with a sigh of relief and let the peace of God warm my heart from its frozen state. I don't understand how it works, but He does it just the same.

The Lord is my shepherd, I lack nothing.

He makes me lie down in green pastures,

He leads me beside quiet waters, He restores my soul.

He guides me along the right paths for His name's sake.

Even though I walk through the darkest valley,

I will fear no evil, for You are with me;

Your rod and Your staff, they comfort me.

You prepare a table before me in the presence of my enemies.

You anoint my head with oil; my cup overflows.

Surely Your goodness and love will follow me all the days of my life,

and I will dwell in the house of the Lord forever.

(Psalm 23, NIV)

"We have each day to be faithful for that one short day,
and long years and a long life will take care of themselves
without the sense of their length or their weight even being a burden."
Andrew Murray

"In the same way, the Spirit helps us in our weakness.
We do not know what we are to pray for,
but the Spirit himself intercedes for us through wordless groans."
(Romans 8:26, ESV)

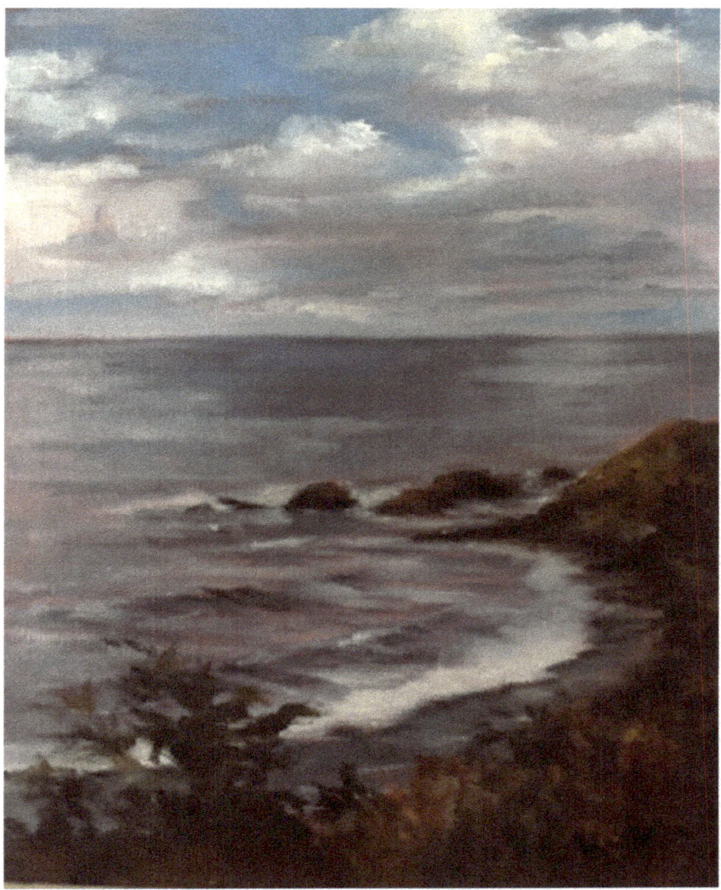

OIL PAINTING, *OREGON COAST* © LEIGH D. FITZ

List Making

February 28, 2010

It's been an interesting weekend full of sickness and self-perceived laziness. I judge myself harshly for not "getting enough done." When I think back, I realize now that I use this phrase a great deal, as both a positive and negative: "I got a lot done," or, "I didn't get much done."

What does it really mean to "get stuff done"? Why must I measure my life or my inner soul by what I achieve, or don't achieve, in the course of a given day? Why is it that I feel good about myself if I have a long list and I'm able to cross everything off? Why should the mundane things that appear on a list—laundry, phone calls, cleaning, shopping, cooking, etc.—cause feelings of accomplishment if completed, or a sense of failure if not?

My dad was known for the three-by-five card he kept in his shirt pocket at all times. He would retrieve it often to add or subtract something from his list of things to be accomplished. He wrote books on time management and strategies for living. He led an organized and disciplined life. Measuring myself by this standard is probably one of the reasons I carry a weight of guilt for my often disorganized life, especially when my list of things to do goes undone.

I want to be organized, like my dad, but I don't want my life to be compartmentalized or measured by a list. And if I do make a list, I want it to be full of life-giving things: watch a sunrise, paint a picture, spend time with family and friends, play with my dog, go hiking, see the beauty in the weather (rain or sun), have a deep conversation that encourages another (which, by doing so encourages me). I want to smile at my husband and tell him the whats and the whys of my love, be aware of God's presence and His voice, pray for a friend or foe, exercise, and marvel at how amazing it is that the body can move in infinite ways—to stretch, breathe deeply, laugh, and relish each moment. In the end, it's the latter list I long to live.

I know JD would also like some of those things on his list too, but the reality is, he still needs to go to work each day in order to make a living and pay the bills. Cooking, cleaning, and yard work still have to be accomplished as well, so how do I achieve balance? I know that if something is not written on my calendar or on my to-do list, it doesn't get accomplished. But I also want to achieve work-life balance, because at the end of my life it will not be the work I've achieved that will bring satisfaction, but rather my time spent nourishing relationships, creating art, and writing—in that order.

If time for meditation, prayer, painting, and exercise are on my calendar, then I see clearly what time remains for the routine. Likewise, my relationships are a priority, so time with people needs to be sprinkled throughout my calendar as well. I know the mundane and the routine must be accomplished, but all too often I don't get to the essential things, because my list of mundane tasks is too long. Maybe I just need to remind myself of what really matters, and make sure those things make the list.

What's on your list today?

My dad's life verse:

"A man's mind plans his way, but the Lord directs his steps."
(Proverbs 16:9, NASB)

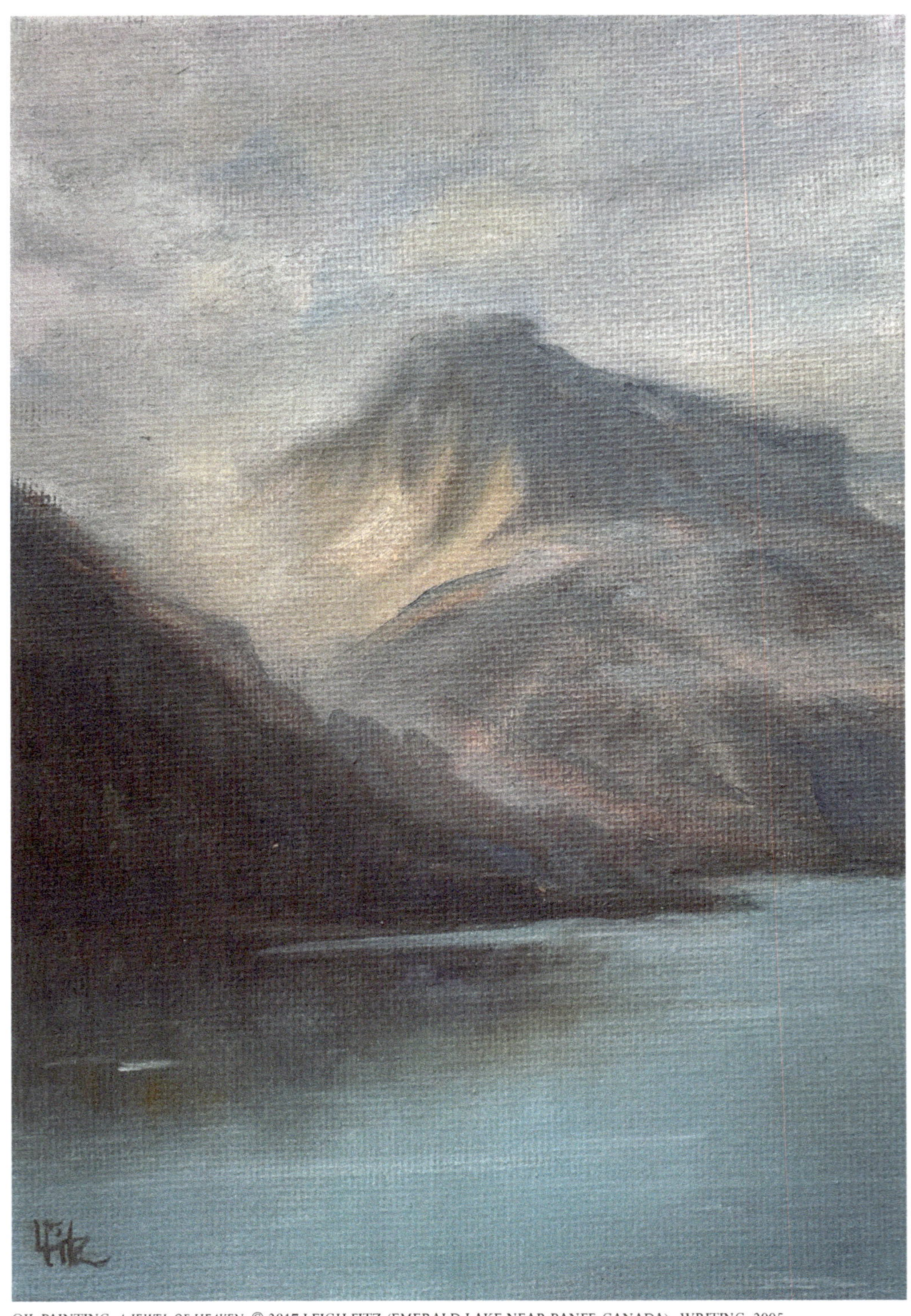

OIL PAINTING, *A JEWEL OF HEAVEN* © 2017 LEIGH FITZ (EMERALD LAKE NEAR BANFF, CANADA) ; WRITING, 2005

A Glimpse of Heaven

Dreams that visit us in the dark hours of the night rarely feel real in the light of day. They fade rapidly, eluding our conscious thoughts. This dream was different. This dream stayed anchored in my mind even years later. This dream forever changed my life.

But let me back up. My hope and comfort of Heaven, while real, has always been tarnished with the fear of suffering and death. Consequently, I only thought of it in the periphery of my life. No longer. This fear vanished as I woke one morning from a dream that was so vividly real I wondered if I might have been with God in another realm. It felt strangely personal, so I didn't speak of it, except to my husband.

But one day, JD encouraged me to share it with my brother-in-law, who in turn told me he thought it was a revelation from God, and that I should write it down to share and encourage others. I hesitated to honor this request, as I didn't feel I had the wherewithal to write it down. So, I asked God to clearly show me whether this was the right course of action.

After this prayer, I turned to my scheduled daily Bible reading for that day, which contained the following verses from Habakkuk: "Then the Lord replied, 'Write down the revelation and make it plain on tablets so that a herald may run with it. For the revelation awaits its appointed time; it speaks of the end, and it will not prove false. Though it lingers, wait for it; it will certainly come and will not delay.'"[11]

It couldn't have been more clear! So, what follows is my revelation, or "dream," if you prefer; you may choose to think of it as you wish. I will make it as plain as I can, but it was anything but plain to me. I pray it will be as encouraging and helpful in conquering your own fears of death as it was for me.

I was driving late into the night, tired from a long day. The narrow road snaked through the utterly dark mountain passes. Weariness and a sense of worry were settling in quickly. These feelings were so potent that I wondered if I would make it home. I needed to stop and close my eyes, even for a few minutes, but no place was available to turn off the road safely. I felt utterly alone, setting off a fear that started to creep into my psyche, a fear that I wouldn't be able to concentrate and drive safely much longer.

11. Habakkuk 2:2-3, NIV

Suddenly, other cars were coming at me quickly with blinding headlights. It became strenuous to stay alert and attentive to the lines of my lane. I felt this burden that life was complicated and stressful. I later reflected that this road felt much like my life: overworked, busy, and fraught with urgent priorities—health problems, broken relationships, concerns, and losses—all like cars and trucks coming rapidly toward me and passing dangerously close in a blinding light. My world was a road with no turn-out lanes for me to rest in, making it too threatening to stop or be still, for fear I would get left behind or be unable to keep up.

As I crested over a hill, there appeared a massive valley to my left, overflowing with marvelous light and panoramic views. I saw meadows filled with light, lakes, mountains, flowers, and a dazzling endless sky, sparkling with intense colors and light that did not come from the sun. It was overwhelmingly gorgeous and unlike anything I had seen or experienced. The colors were different—intense yet softly textured, with a feeling and quality I still find impossible to describe.

Suddenly, my desire to get home was gone, and my weariness and loneliness vanished. I was captivated. But it became too difficult to both drive and explore what I was seeing. When I turned to look back at the road, I was immediately blinded by the white light of the oncoming vehicles, preventing me from seeing the heavenly place any longer. The road I was on took every ounce of my energy to travel safely.

But the vision was positively enticing, filling me with joy—and looking away from it brought only darkness, cold, and hollowness to my soul. I knew that if I was going to stay alive, I needed to force myself to concentrate with every drop of focus I possessed to keep from crashing into the oncoming vehicles or going off the edge into oblivion. Yet I was compelled to look at this life-giving view to my left! I had to choose between "life" on this dark, burdensome road, and exploring the heavenly vision I had seen.

The choice was no longer difficult. I knew that death would surely come if I took my eyes off the road, but even more than that, I knew I had to see this glorious, peace-filled place. So, I chose death in order to see the "life" that awaited on my left.

The next moment (if it was even long enough to be called a moment), I was lifted into the air. In a word, "flying" is as close as I can come to describing my state, but I had no sense of air flow, heat, or cold, just an exquisite touch. Jesus was all around me. I asked Him to take me higher and show me more, and I soared in His power. I took in with all my heightened senses this perfect world—with unfamiliar sounds like pleasant music, and these incredible views that I could touch.

"Lord, take me higher," were the words that kept coming to my lips. And He did, into the heavens, yet still on Earth, examining new colors and varieties of flowers. I was given a gift, an ability to see everything and anything all in the same moment, and my eyes had an expanded visual acuity to see minute details of objects miles away. There are no words that I can accurately use to describe the pleasant sensation running through my entire body except to call it an overwhelmingly delightful feeling of ecstasy that I knew would never end.

Jesus was all around me. I was overwhelmed with His magnificence and His presence, yet so "at home" and relaxed as well. It is the closest I've ever come to what I imagine is pure perfection, saturated with joy. As we soared up higher and higher, I looked up to the highest mountain pinnacle and saw God (in my dream, I somehow knew it was Him), enfolding me into His arms. His gaze was on me, full of compassion, filled with more significance than any love I had ever known. It was as if I were the center of His universe. I was with God, yet still in the air with Jesus at the same time. He loved me and was loving me so completely. The experience of being cherished wholeheartedly was powerfully satisfying. I've never felt so loved and adored.

I awoke with a smile, yet longed to return to the dream. My life was now forever punctuated with the assurance that Heaven exists and that God loves me thoroughly. Words could never come close, even if I had a lifetime to write every thought, memory, and feeling of this dream-revelation.

To capture this dream on canvas is an impossibility but I've often thought to make the attempt. This thumbnail painting (from a picture I took in Canada) was just an experiment to render a greater painting in the future. *A Jewel of Heaven* is not what I saw necessarily, but reminds me of the unusual color of the water—emerald green.

How could one dream change me forever? How can one dream be as or more real than life itself? The beauty of Heaven was undoubtedly a feast for the eyes, but experiencing God's presence and to dwell in His total love for me was everything. That's Heaven—no fear, no anxiety, no pain, no concern even for this world I had left behind—just the sensation of being flooded with laughter and an unrivaled love. I have no doubt that God gave me this dream to give me a glimpse of Heaven and forever erase any fear of the future.

I pray that God's love will become plain to you on your highway, too.

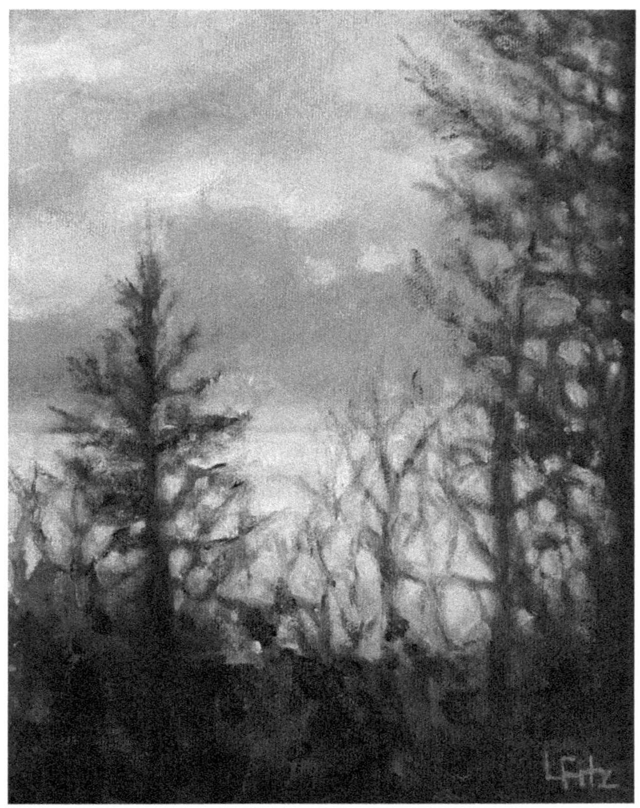

UNFINISHED PAINTING, *PAINTING IN THE DARK*, © 2018 LEIGH D. FITZ

Colors of My Palette

My Prayer

Lord, I struggle to find the good in the day, as I wake to significant pain. Discouragement arrives so abruptly that I close my eyes to any possibility of light. So, I'm asking You—my only hope—how do I live with a grateful heart in a wounded body? How do I get past the pain in order to grasp all the graces and goodness You've lavished on me? How do I live in the dark when I can't find my way? How do I paint a sunrise when there are only shades of gray on my palette?

I trust and rely on You. Easy to say, easy to write, words I believe, yet even if I have the right answers it doesn't always make the darkness turn to light. So, I guess I've learned to live this day, this one day, faithfully, and if that's too difficult, I will put my focus on just one hour, leaning into Your grace, believing that You hold me tight.

"Life unfolds as a mystery, an enterprise whose outcome cannot be foretold. We do not get what we expect. We stumble on cracks, are faced with imperfection, bonds tested and tightened. And our landscapes shift in sunshine and in shade. There is light. There is. Look for it. Look for it shining over your shoulder on the past. It was light where you went once. It was light where you are now. It will be light where you will go again."

(Jennifer Worth)

It is easy to slip into worry when I feel like I'm being crushed by the weight of darkness. The Bible directs us, when walking in the dark, to trust in God. I wholeheartedly believe this, yet I'm trying to discover just what that "trust" and "relying" look like in my everyday life, when the darkness falls heavy as the sun is rising. As I view my life through the lens of gratefulness, even in difficulties, my vision can be transformed.

When I begin a painting, I always start with the darkest colors, laying in the lines of the composition. Then I move to the mid-tones and, finally, to the lightest colors. Shadows aid the bright light colors in a way they can't perform on their own accord. Placing the darkest dark next to the lightest light on canvas draws the eye from the dark to the light, creating the illusion that the light is brighter than it actually is on its own.

I'm handing my dark, gray day over to God just now, and as the weight internally shifts and is redistributed, color comes to my eyes and warmth to my soul. The light of Hope is coming. I see it!

"Remember your word to your servant; you have given me hope through it.
This is my comfort in my affliction; your promise has given me life…
I rise before dawn and cry for help; I put my hope in your word."
(Psalm 119:49-50 and 119:147, HCSB)

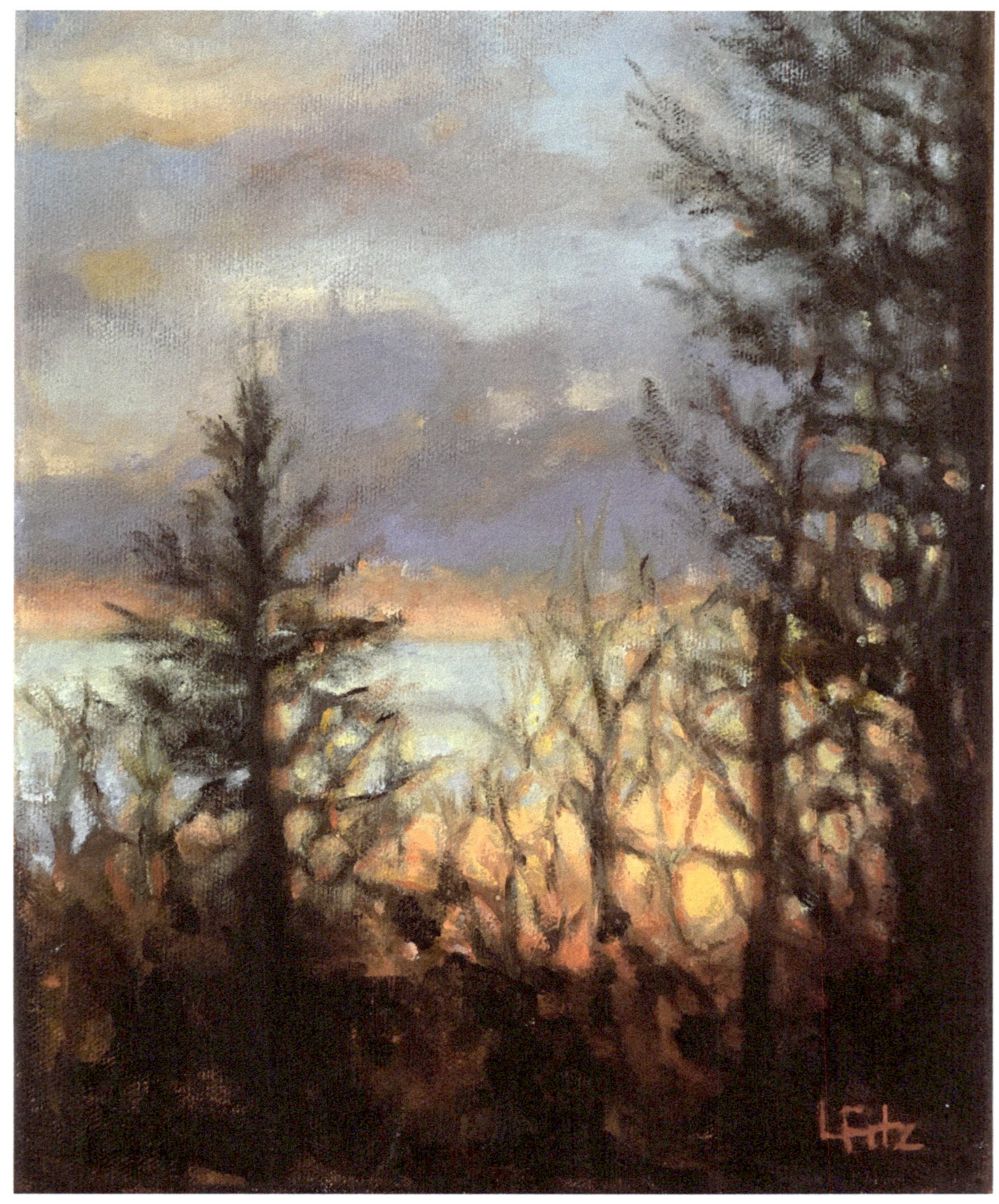

PAINTING, *PAINTING IN THE DARK*, © 2018 LEIGH D. FITZ; WRITING, MARCH 2017

Weeping with God

"You keep track of all my sorrows. You have collected all my tears in your bottle.

You have recorded each one in your book."

(Psalms 56:8, NLT)

I've often contemplated why it is that God "collects our tears." I wonder if our tears are thoughts or emotions that only God can interpret. Are tears a form of communication between my heart and God's? I believe so. He keeps these tears and holds them especially close, remembering my tears of profound sorrow, joy, and gratefulness. He remembers.

Tears, all through Scripture, seem to "move" the heart of God in a mysterious way. It's as if He listens more closely because our honest selves are "spilling" out—not just reciting words we've been taught, but because the heart is uttering profound thoughts or feelings that words fail to describe.

Tears sometimes arrive before tangible thoughts, warning me that unresolved hurt, or loss that hasn't been sufficiently grieved, is rising to the surface. These tears before Him are precious, and He bends down and catches them as they fall. When we weep, we speak with our hearts, and God stops to listen.

It's been in those times of tears that I've been met with the most intimate of encounters. It's unexplainable. It's indescribable. It's as if God were crying too, and His tears drench me with grace in an unspeakable, healing way. It's in these moments, I've experienced the tenderness of my Father, the loving expressions on the face of Jesus, and the utter peacefulness of the Holy Spirit.

I jotted down these words and emailed them to myself as I waited for the results of my mammogram. It's not characteristic of me to write in public, but surrounded by other women whom I imagine were worried about their own results, and sensing a somber atmosphere, I felt compelled to pen these words. When a doctor came to talk to me, I pressed send and turned my phone off. I was told there was an abnormality that needed to be biopsied immediately. I had been told the same thing the year prior when they discovered the cancer. I felt like I had been punched in the gut by dread.

On the way home, in the car, my sobs overtook me. As I pulled off the road, I gasped, "PLEASE God, NO, not again!" My words shot out between gulps of breath, as I allowed my mind to go down the frenzied trail of "what ifs." When I arrived home and had dried my tears, I sat down to read the words I had written at my appointment. Tears started all over again, but this time they came from a place of trust. He was catching every tear, which meant He was very close.

When I gaze through eyes filled with tears, everything looks blurred, but somehow, I see God's compassionate nature more clearly.

"Weeping may tarry for the night, BUT joy comes in the morning."
(Psalm 30:5, NIV)

"Arise, cry out in the night, as the watches of the night begin;
pour out your heart like water in the presence of the Lord."
(Lamentations 2:19, NIV)

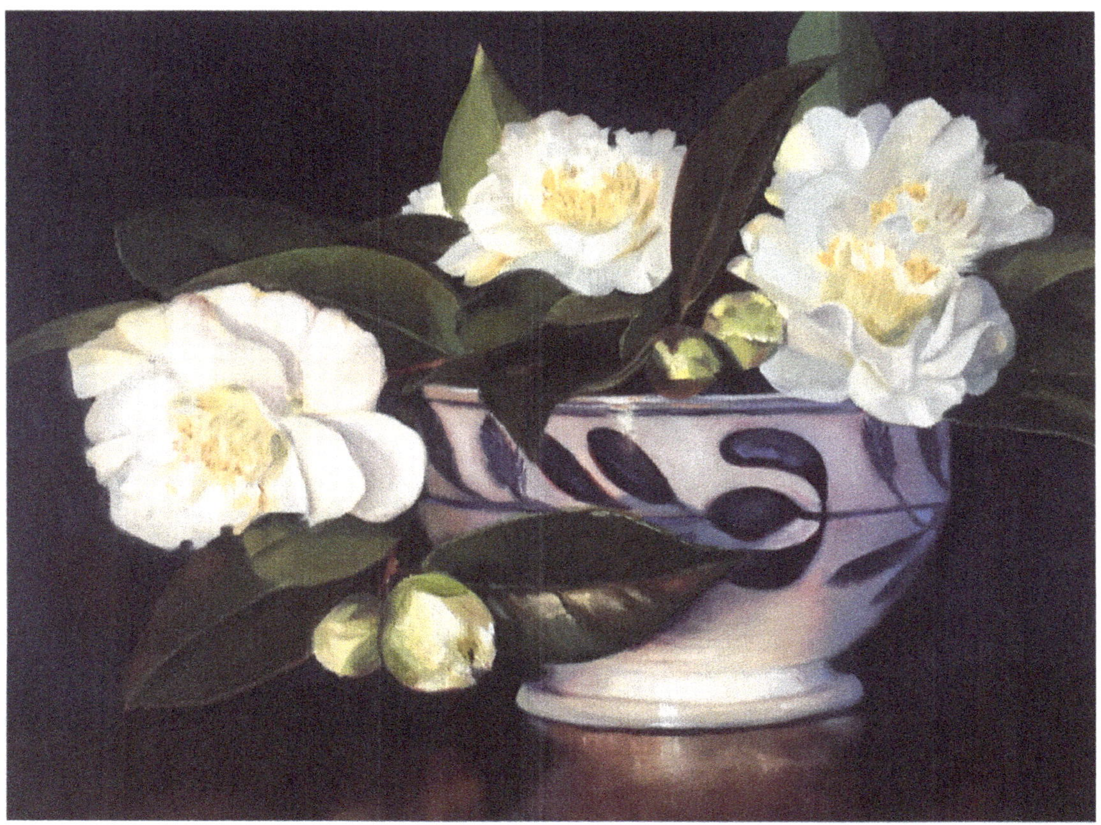

OIL PAINTING, A WINTER'S GIFT © 1999 LEIGH D. FITZ

Gifts Given in the Dark

Sorrow and grief can wrap themselves tightly around the core of my being and relentlessly hold my heart captive. Long winters of darkness can cause me to lose hope that spring will ever return. It was during one of these times in my life that I was inspired to paint *A Winter's Gift*.

When I look at this painting, I'm reminded of the bright spots, or gifts, that emerge from the dark winters of my life. I purposely painted the background black and the camellias white to represent the great contrast that exists in life. It's a reminder to focus on the bright light of goodness and beauty rather than the darkness of loss.

The camellias had surprised me by blooming early in February, when winter was hardly over. My garden looked bare and bleak, with the exception of these white buds bursting with blooms in contrast to the dark winter day. I picked some of them to bring hope into the house, and as I painted these beauties I thought about my own personal "winter of loss."

A prolonged double ear infection and exposure to loud noises had caused tinnitus in my ears. As the condition worsened, it was becoming increasingly difficult to interpret the human voice, which I longed to hear clearly. The sounds of nature, such as the sweet song of birds chirping, fell silent. Without a hint of sympathy, my doctor told me there was nothing to be done for the ringing and that over time I would continue to lose more of my hearing.

As my tears started falling, the doctor made his exit, taking with him the last bit of hope I had left. (Come on, people—tears are silent words that should be acknowledged!) Hearing aids only turned up the volume of distracting sounds and drowned the voices of the people I valued most. I felt alone, withdrawing from life more and more as the tinnitus increased and language I had lived with grew more and more foreign sounding .

To make matters worse, this was a hidden loss. No sympathy cards arrived at my door. People couldn't remember to modify their speaking patterns. I couldn't tolerate loud noises such as restaurants, parties, or church services. Silence became what I craved, yet in silence the ringing was more pronounced, and stole sleep and peace from me as I navigated migraines and exhaustion.

No surprise; I developed quite a grumpy spirit as well. As the ringing grew more relentless, I grew more irritable and realized I needed to find a way to grieve my loss without falling headlong into a deep hole of bitterness. Clearly, we all have or will experience loss, but I hadn't anticipated that mine would arrive in my thirties when so much life was still to come. Resentment sprouted like weeds as I focused on what I lacked, instead of my gains. But, what I have discovered through these many years of living with tinnitus and hearing decline is the surprising beauty of "winter" in my life. Sometimes I even find that spring arrives before winter's end, and that my gains can outweigh my groans.

When this journey of tinnitus and hearing loss began, I first asked God to heal me. I politely prayed for God to take away the insane ringing but I was met with silence (actually, I was met by ongoing and even worsening ringing). I asked other people to pray for me in hopes that God would listen to them. When that didn't work, I started begging, pleading with many tears for God to take away the agony. When He didn't respond to my sadness, I met him with anger and pounding fists. I questioned Him about how He could call himself loving yet let me suffer. Lastly, I tried bargaining with Him, telling Him that if He healed me I'd certainly give Him the credit.

It was after this last request that God answered me through a verse in 2 Corinthians 12:9, "My grace is sufficient for you, for my power is made perfect in weakness." At the time, it was a difficult pill to swallow, but God came through with His promise. He mysteriously planted new gifts of grace. His power within me brought good growth in so many ways. The greatest gift was the intimacy I felt toward God as He tenderly cared for me through the dark days with an encouraging Scripture verse or a kind word from a family member or friend. My tinnitus became a reminder of God's constant love for me personally. My other senses were heightened and compensated for the one sense that struggled. Honestly, I don't think I would have clung to God or pursued Him so desperately if it were not for this loss.

I wonder too, if I would have started painting or if I would have valued my sight as much as I do without my personal "winter." Hearing impairment has heightened my awareness of the loss that others are living with (especially hidden agonies), and has given me a deep desire to listen to their stories and pray for them. It's a paradox; there's nothing more I would rather live without than tinnitus and hearing loss, but at the same time I would not want to be without these valued companions that keep instructing and tutoring me through life. These "gifts" don't negate the losses, but they wrap a cozy blanket around my heart and soul as I wait for the promise of a greater, eternal spring to come.

"Three times I pleaded with the Lord to take it away from me. But he said to me,

"My grace is sufficient for you, for my power is made perfect in weakness.

Therefore I will boast all the more gladly about my weaknesses,

so that Christ's power may rest on me. That is why, for Christ's sake,

I delight in weaknesses, in insults, in hardships, in persecutions, in difficulties.

For when I am weak, then I am strong."

(2 Corinthians 12:8-10, NIV)

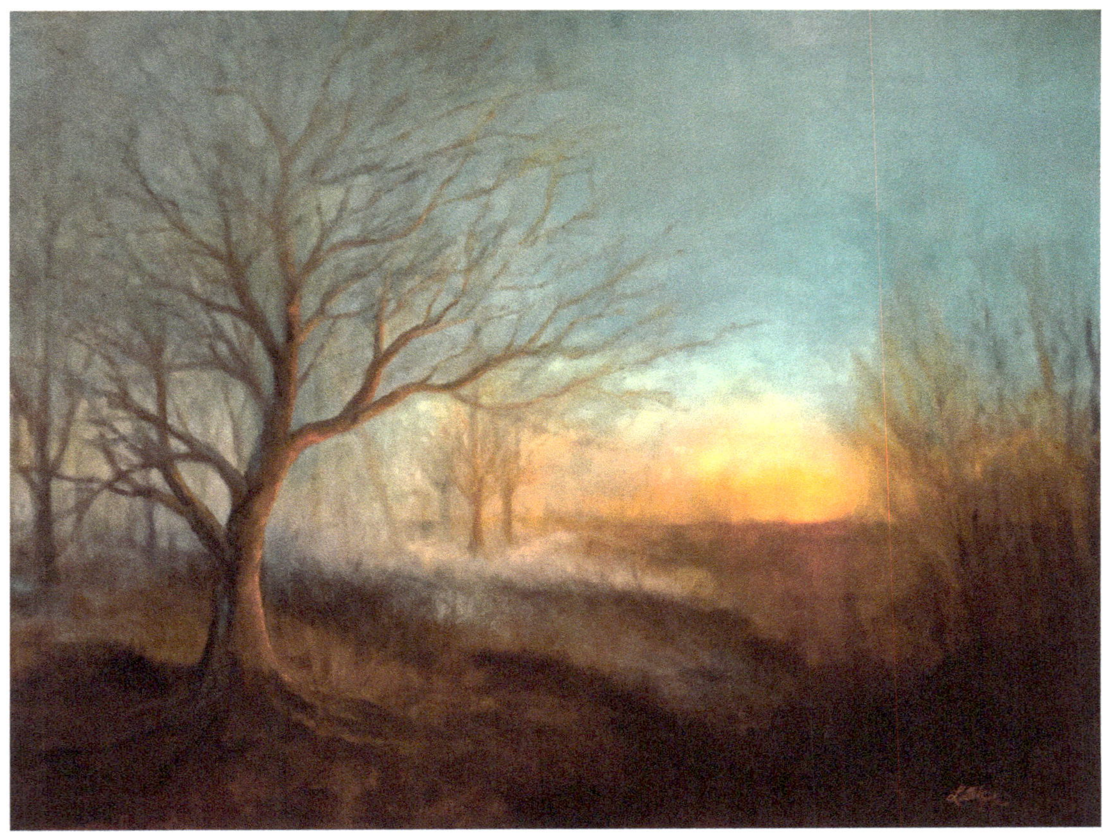

OIL PAINTING, *WINTER'S END* © 2010 LEIGH D. FITZ; WRITING, 2007 AND 2013

Winter's End

Journal Entry, 2010

Yesterday was a long day of struggle, a day to do battle with both my emotions and with my paintbrush.

At present, I'm working on a three-by-four-foot canvas. I'm painting purely from my head, which I'm re-alizing now was probably a bad idea. It's for my daughter, Kate, so I want it to be beautiful, but that comes with a lot of pressure that I place on myself. I reworked the sunrise no less than five times just yesterday!

I love to paint, but sometimes it's complicated by my self-criticism. I want her to like it, but I'm not sure I like it yet. Anyway, while painting, I said out loud, "Will I be able to resurrect this?" I had a similar feeling about myself this morning. "Will I be able to come out of this hiding place of sadness—this cold tomb of self-doubt and self-pity.?"

In that moment of reflection, I wondered if this painting should be called *Winter's End: The Resurrection of Our Lives.* I thought about how God breathes life into my tired spirit, resurrecting me from the bleakness of my thoughts with His warm light. He gives me life and keeps renewing my soul each day as I sit with Him in the morning. I am reminded of the old hymn, "The Steadfast Love of the Lord," that speaks of this renewal: "The steadfast love of the Lord never ceases, his mercies never come to an end; they are new every morning—great is thy faithfulness."[12]

Six Years Later

In the barrenness of winter—when my soul is cold and hungry—God arrives, drenching me in warm rays of sunlight, feeding me with His love and compassion. Hope is delivered. But, truthfully, hope isn't always as distinguishable as a sunrise—at least it doesn't seem to reach where I'm hiding in the dark.

Who hears my thoughts? Who sees my tears soak into my pillow? Who cares that my companion is loneliness? Condemnation and guilt accompany me as well, letting me know that they seriously doubt that God is in my reach. Despair and depression can visit me in times of plenty, even on a summer day. I'm not sure why; I only know the surety that it is so. If I allow them to stay or entertain them in any way (despair and depression, that is), I turn inward and head down into a bottomless pit where blackness dwells, to hide from family and friends.

I've convinced myself that being in a depressed state of mind is not acceptable, and, if exposed to family or friends, I will be thought of as weak, unlovable, and untrusting of God. Thankfully, though, I have come to believe God not only sees me, but He makes His way down into the depths to sit beside me, to comfort. Being aware of His presence calms me, yet even still, often I refuse to budge, and I wallow in self-pity.

I'm attempting to put away all these thoughts as I start my day. It feels as if the air is too thick with anxiety for me to breathe. *Shake it off, Leigh,* I tell myself. *Get up, get going; have something to show for your day.* But I stay here glued to my chair, feeling hopeless. I feel as if my spirit is crushed into dust that then collects all over the "furniture" of my life. I'm a mess. *Lord, come to me, hold me, fill the gaps in my broken state. Mend my soul. Give me energy and help to emerge from my hiding place.*

12. from Lamentations 3:20

No solutions today . . . so I decide to carefully close my journal with all these penned emotions and prayers and tuck it away in a drawer, tidy up, paste a smile on my face, and leave these feelings for another time.

Minutes after writing this last journal entry, as I was in the shower, I started weeping uncontrollably. I was coming undone. I cried out to God and begged Him to pray for me because I couldn't do it myself. But then I said, "I need You to pray for me with 'skin on.' Please have somebody call me, not ask questions, and just pray for me." I turned off the shower and reached for a towel, just as my phone started ringing. I wondered whom God had prompted to call me. Amazed, I had never made this request of Him before.

My voice struggled and faltered as I said the word, "Hello," immediately alerting my daughter, Kate, who had made the call, to my distress. She anxiously asked if I was okay. I was honest—telling her simply without explanation that I wasn't doing well, but that I thought God Himself had prompted her to call to pray for me. Without hesitation or any more questions, she immediately started praying for me over the phone. She even used the imagery of a bottomless pit, which I had imagined as well. She assured me of God's presence with me. She prayed the promises of God into my life, reminding me of His love. And then we said our goodbyes. No questions asked—no added words except, "I love you, Mom."

I am overwhelmed every time I think of how God tenderly spoke a loving prayer for me through the voice of my daughter that day in my bathroom, as the water dripped down my face, mingling with my tears, washing away the dust of sadness, restoring my joy and belief in His love. His capability to hear my cries for help with such clarity, even in the shower, baffles me still.

Later that day, Kate sent me the following scripture in a text message: "I waited patiently for the Lord, and He turned to me and heard my cry. He lifted me out of the slimy pit, out of the mud and mire; he set my feet on a rock and gave me a firm place to stand. He put a new song in my mouth, a hymn of praise to our God. Many will see and fear and put their trust in the Lord."[13] I can't say I was patiently waiting for the Lord but I do know He heard my cry for help and pulled me out of the slimy pit of hopelessness and showered me off with His tender mercy.

Today

Now as I gaze at this painting that hangs in Kate's home, I see the Light has arrived and found this crooked tree; transformation has begun. It feels like this tree is bending toward the light, striving to see hope on the horizon, wanting to reflect the sun's rays where warmth comes to bring life. Yet, there remains a dark pit as well. Is there

13. Psalm 40:1-4, NIV

a choice that needs to be made? A choice to take my eyes off the "pit of scarcity or self-pity," and look upwards? This painting speaks of hope and the rebirth of a life as "spring" arrives and "winter" comes to an end.

" . . . because of the tender mercy of God, by which the rising sun will come to us

from heaven to shine on those living in darkness, and the shadow of death,

to guide our feet into the path of peace."

(Luke 1:78-79, NIV)

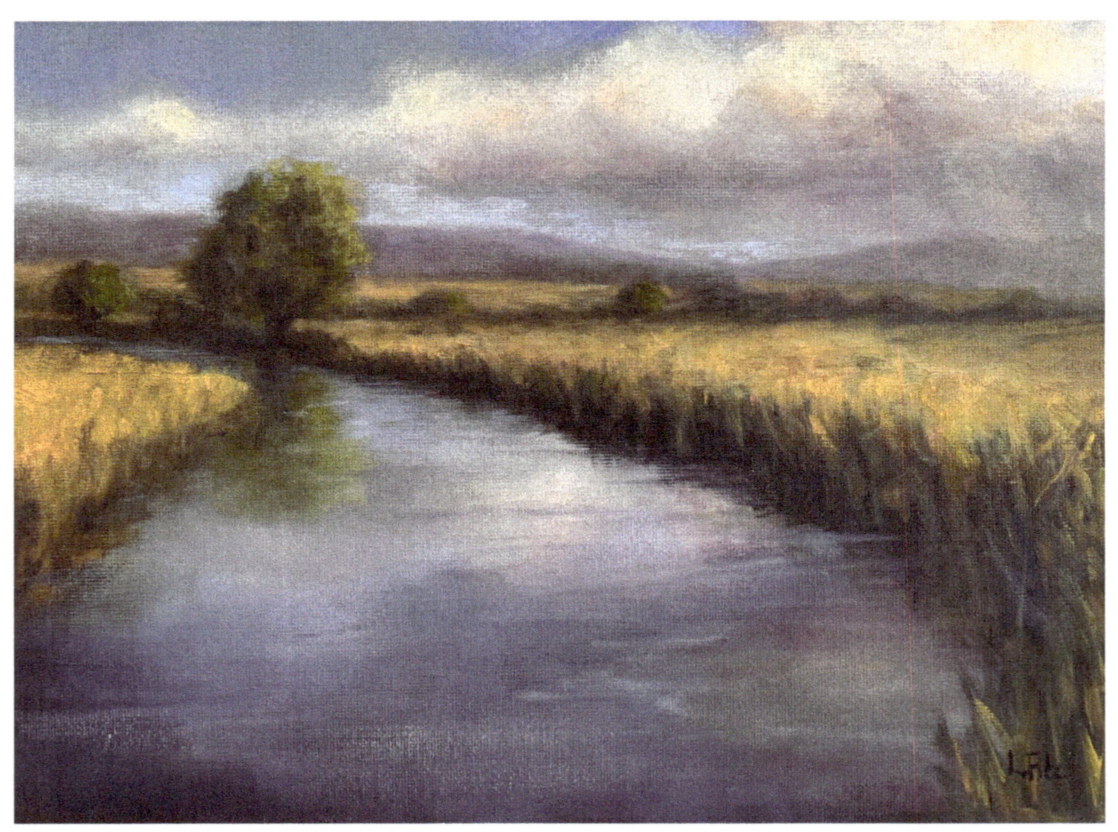

OIL PAINTING, *GO WITH THAT FLOW* © 2019 LEIGH D. FITZ

Springs

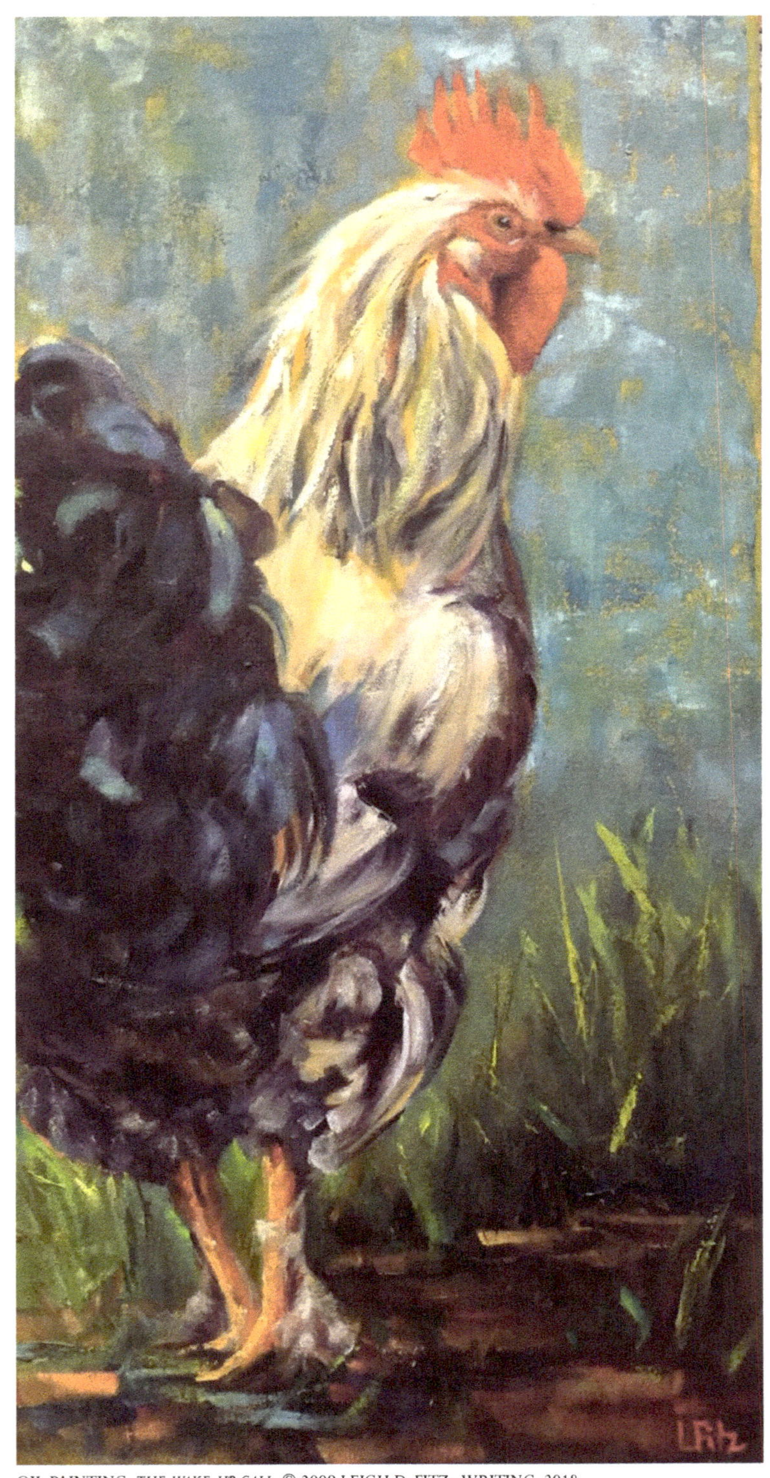

OIL PAINTING, *THE WAKE-UP CALL* © 2009 LEIGH D. FITZ; WRITING, 2018

The Wake-up Call

In retrospect, I think I must have been dozing—nodding off, so to speak, from life itself. I was too sleepy at first to hear the "wake-up call," because I had slipped into complacency. I just wanted to continue to take my ease in life. I had even written in my journal that I was feeling a bit bored. I'm not tired or bored now. I'm terrified!

Today I found out that I have *cancer*. Now that's a word that wakes you up! It's a diagnosis I have to face head on and take seriously. There is no taking my ease with life anymore. I am allowing this word, *cancer*, to seep into my psyche, knowing it will bring a new perspective to my life. I'm holding it as I would a valuable object. The person I am will begin again, being reshaped to think and act differently than before. I'm leaving the "Before Cancer" self (BC) behind and am entering through a new door: "After Diagnosis" (AD). It feels like the door behind me is now securely locked; there is no returning to the person I used to be.

Despite the fear and uncertainty I am feeling, I sense I'm on a sacred journey, and I want to be acutely aware of what I learn along the way. I have a brand new journal and pen, and I'm sitting poised, wide awake, ready to take dictation on what I hear and feel. I'm just hoping I'm not too fearful or exhausted to notice the good that still exists in my life while experiencing the losses.

Two Weeks AD

This new AD life is a rough road—inconvenient, time-consuming, as well as mentally, emotionally, and even spiritually exhausting. Imagining the "what ifs" and worst-case scenarios is a death sentence for my emotional stability and for my heart. Fear swoops in and grabs my hope with its powerful claws and flies away in seconds. It's in those moments I hear my voice crying out to God for help.

About a Month AD

When I heard the nurse say, "Unfortunately, you have Invasive Ductal Cell Carcinoma," life immediately felt differ-ent, as if the temperature had suddenly dropped and a dense fog had settled around me. My vision felt skewed. Life as I knew it fell away. Time stopped. My mind screamed, *No, no, this isn't me she's talking about—wrong person, wrong chart.* Yet my heart simultaneously said, *Yes, I already know; God has prepared me for this moment. He already taught me that His grace is more than sufficient in trials.* A calming peace was also present in that room. I knew God was listening to every word and that He heard my heart, gracing me with peace and hope.

That same morning of my diagnosis, by God's grace, I awoke with a specific verse on my heart: "Hope does not disappoint, for the love of God is poured out in our hearts by the Holy Spirit, who is given to us."[14] A mysteriously beautiful cherishing hope. Not a death sentence, but one of life: "Praise be to the God and Father of our Lord Jesus Christ! In His great mercy He has given us new birth into a living hope through the resurrection of Jesus Christ from the dead, and into an inheritance, which can never perish, spoil, or fade, kept in heaven for you."[15] This life sentence of a living hope in heaven fills me now even though I'm still on earth. I experienced it on my diagnosis day, and I continue to experience it today. It didn't negate my grief or sadness, rather it helped me not to fear the future. God graced me with His word, gifting me peace to sit alongside my sadness, joining hands with hope.

1.5 Months AD

Still, the "fog" remains. I struggle to remember scheduled events or the simple fact that others around me have needs too. I'm becoming more self-consumed than I ever remember. Life feels complicated by doctors' appointments, surgeries, waiting for results, side effects—always side effects from surgery and medication. I wouldn't have chosen these "colors" for my palette right now. I don't sleep well—the pain and these new hot flashes leave me short-tempered, discouraged, and downright grumpy. As I stand in this fog that seems to grow denser by the day, I can't really see the people near me. I can't tell which direction I should go. Sometimes hope is invisible. Cancer is lonely. Yet, I believe God is in this fog, and He sees me even if my vision is obscured. God holds me even when my unbelief is waving in the breeze of illness.

Two Months AD

Obviously, I did not want cancer. The shock of the word, attached to my name, led me to denial. After the initial shock and denial came tears of grief. I wept until, seemingly, no tears were left. Slowly, I began to feel open to a loving God pruning my life, cutting and trimming back those places that had "unruly" growth—the pride and other "dead" areas of discontent and self-centeredness. *Will this make me healthier?* I wondered.

How do I trust in God when all I can see through the fog is the sharp edge of the knife? How do I find peace when I am trembling? How do I focus on the goodness of God's word as I read the literature of my disease? Wrestling

14. Romans 5:5
15. 1 Peter 1:3

with these and other such questions fatigues me, so I'm simply opening my hands and praying for God to do His creative artwork on my soul as I remember, "We are God's workmanship, created in Christ Jesus to do good works, which God prepared in advance for us to do."[16]

2.5 Months AD

I feel undone and depleted today. Spiritually, I'm wavering. I hate cancer. A sadness lives deep within me that feels suffocating. Some days I don't have the strength or the power to throw it off me, and I fear it will bury me alive.

"Oh Lord, I am trying to trust You, but help me with my lack of trust. I believe in You, but help me with my unbelief. Comfort me, heal me; I am in serious trouble. I'm asking for Your favor on me and lift these exhausting symptoms. Hear my desperate cry for help. Please don't be silent. Where are You? I'm calling for Your great love and comfort to wash off on me."

3 Months AD

A peace that could only be from God has settled on me since I penned the last entry. I believe God answered my cry for help. The circumstances haven't changed a bit, only my attitude. Fear and anxiety have been drained out, replaced by a peaceful presence. "Thank you, Father God, for your compassion and love."

3.5 Months AD

Radiation. When harsh circumstances come my way, I just want to get through them as quickly as possible and get on with living. My days with radiation and cancer drugs seem to be a waste of time. What if I don't get well? Or what if all the symptoms and side effects from radiation and the drug therapy just continue? Do I just wait until I feel well enough to start living? Yesterday, I seemed to get an answer; I realized that this is my life, and I need to live it to the fullest today. Even while I'm sick. Especially while I'm sick! I don't have any assurance that my health will be good in the future, but I do have the guarantee that God's grace will be sufficient today and each day going forward.

Next Day

After yesterday's entry, I made the decision to stop waiting to get well and to start living now. Though I had had a difficult night with little sleep and I awoke with a headache, I went to my painting class anyway. I wrote a couple of notes of encouragement to others. I went to radiation, came home, and made a simple dinner for six friends

16. Ephesians 2:10

and had a great evening. This was a good day even if I wasn't feeling my best physically. I want to celebrate all that God has done and all that He will do BEFORE I get well.

4 Months AD

I am almost done with radiation. It has stolen all my energy, so I'm napping every day, wondering if I'll ever be capable of doing the ordinary things in life again. In the midst of these feelings of inadequacy, my daughter Kate responded that Moses had questioned God's plan to use him, asking "Who am I?". God replied by telling Moses who *He* was, not who Moses was. He described himself as "I Am Who I Am," the dependable and powerful God who desires our trust and wants us to keep our eyes fixed on Him, not ourselves. I knew there was great truth in what she was saying. I didn't have the luxury to consider whether I was capable of dealing with cancer or future events. I needed to focus on God's capability instead.

"Lord, help me to keep trusting and believing who you are-even on the days, like today, when I'm tired, head-achy, and discouraged, thinking that it's going to end badly."

4.5 Months AD

Over the last few months, as I have walked through this steep valley, I have found myself "picking things up" like memory stones along the way. Because it was dark for so long, I wasn't sure just what I had placed in the various pockets of my heart. But now that I have emerged back into the light, I realize that my pockets are filled with treasures I have found, or perhaps, been given by another. I was given gold in the depths of the valley, and lots of it. There are treasures to be had in the darkness!

As I examine them, I notice that my fears of loss and of being spewed out as "less of a woman" were needless. Instead, I found the truth was quite the opposite. My heart was stretched as wisdom was dispensed alongside my medicines. My hearing was improved because "valley acoustics" enhanced my reception of God's voice. My pockets were filled with gratefulness and a more profound love for others. My emotions were disciplined as I learned that worrying about a list of potential adverse outcomes—loss of a breast, loss of hair, the pain of chemotherapy, radiation, surgery, scars both physical and emotional, fear that I would end up as less of a woman (or worse, dead) was disabling me. As most of these things didn't occur, I realized that I was robbing myself of the joys of living each day. My deepened sense of God's presence lathered my soul with a restoring salve.

It's not that I ever desired cancer, but I'm grateful for it and I relish the intimacy of God and the "gifts" given to me in cancer's valley, lessons not fully learned as yet but experienced—a practical "hands-on" experience that taught me how to walk in the darkness of life. That's a gift.

In that extreme darkness, when there was no light, I had to stand still and in that stillness experience God in a way I never could have in the light. Trust expanded, worries diminished, and hope broke free from being buried by heaps of anxiety and fret. My eyes adjusted to the dark as my pupils widened and saw that God, who was so very close all along, stood there facing me with open arms. Like Lazarus, I had "fallen asleep,"[17] and, through cancer, Jesus came to me, to wake me up by showing me His love and instructing me on living life intentionally. And now, living life AD, I can affirm with more certainty the truth of God's presence: "Let the beloved of the Lord rest secure in him, for he will shield him all day long, and the one whom the Lord loves rests between his shoulders."[18]

Much Later AD

Now, in my life AD, this book that I have dreamt of writing for years has a deadline! I want to tell this and other stories, and illustrate them with my paintings, because I now trust God more completely with my work, and I want to release it to Him. I know far better now than ever before that God has been present with me my whole life, both BC and AD. With this confidence, I can approach the tough questions: How do I want to live my last years? What's really important to me? What am I going to do differently? Is there anything I'm doing that doesn't seem profitable? I have truly awakened from a life of "ho-hum" to the thrill of "seeing God so close." And I'm so grateful for my "wake-up call."

Oh Lord, keep me from going back to sleep. Keep me alert to what You want me to do today and each day. I don't want to "doze off" even for a minute. I'm not pressing the "snooze" button anymore!

"I will give you hidden treasures, which is stored in secret places, so that you may know that I am the LORD, the God of Israel, who summoned you by name."
(Isaiah 45:3, NIV)

17. John 11:11
18. Deuteronomy 33:12

The Seed of Discontentment

My husband is constantly at war with weeds. One particularly invasive species, which I planted a few years ago, required a concerted year-long effort to eliminate once it had spread throughout one of our garden beds. All from one ground cover plant! I thought its green leaves and flowers would beautifully complement the other plants, but instead its hidden roots sought out and destroyed its unsuspecting neighbors, choking the life out of them from beneath the soil.

In the same way, planting or allowing an invasive species into my heart's garden and letting it take root can choke out the beautiful flowers of kindness, contentment, understanding, and gentleness. I can allow one critical comment to get rooted in my thoughts in the morning, nurture it through the afternoon, and by evening it has produced a full-grown shade tree of discontentment and doubt. So, I am asking myself today, *How do I keep seeds of discontent from taking root? And secondly, how do I keep from sprinkling seeds of discontent and criticism in other people's "gardens"?*

Recently, a dear friend sent me a kind and encouraging card—and also enclosed an article on how to help damaged hair. She complimented me on something else unrelated, but the negative canceled the positive and left me feeling unsettled and insecure about my hair. I had been trying to focus on inner beauty as the outward fades quickly with age, and I didn't want to get caught up obsessing about my graying hair or my saggy skin. Instead, I had been focusing on growing compassion, kindness, contentment, and a gentle spirit. But I let this one comment erase the positive and "invade" my thoughts and confidence. She wanted to help me, but I took it as a cutting criticism and let it fester within my heart.

This morning, as I was scanning a full parking lot for a space, rain pouring down from above, I failed to see two people attempting to cross in front of me. I only noticed them as I passed because one of the women threw up her hands in frustration, anger, and disdain and pointed to her friend, who was on a knee scooter. Of course, I felt horrible, mainly because my mind was on other (not so important) things, such as an empty parking space nearby. I could have hit them! When I realized they were heading into the store that I was visiting, I almost decided just to go home. Instead, I parked and walked to the store, hoping I wouldn't run into them, but rounding the corner of the first aisle, there they were. Taking a deep breath, I faced the women that I had wronged and said, "Would you please forgive me for my failure to let you cross? I was being careless. I'm truly sorry." The woman who had been angry surprised me with a big hug and a smile and thanked me for taking the time to apologize.

I gathered a few things I needed (and others that I had convinced myself I needed) and headed to the checkout line. The cashier complimented me on my coordinated wrapping paper, ribbon, and holiday boxes that I was purchasing and then said, with a sigh, "I hope someday I, too, will get my act together." I told her not to be fooled by the wrapping paper. (Little did she know I almost mowed down a crippled person in the parking lot!) We both laughed and I took a moment to give her encouragement.

I contemplated both these interactions on my way home. Life is so fragile, and in a single moment, by a simple misstep, I can unintentionally hurt people and cause them discontentment. One woman saw me as careless and unkind; another woman saw me as friendly and having my life together, all within the span of just a few minutes. My takeaway? I need to be honest about the person I am. I need to admit that how I appear to others isn't always who I am or want to be—I have missing parts, I've made mistakes, and under the external "wrappings," I don't have it together.

And, when it comes to evaluating others, I need to remind myself that everyone else experiences failure as well as the desire to be better in some way. I, too, get thrown off by the external wrappings of a person and their comments (like the article about damaged hair), rather than looking at the person within and trying to make their day better. I want to remember what I recently heard: "Be kind, for everyone you meet is fighting a hard battle."

The third takeaway for me that day was noticing how good I felt by asking for forgiveness and taking the time to be kind to someone who felt frustrated with life (and probably with me). Both interactions gave me life—one by being forgiven and one by being thanked, and by being my authentic self. And I thought running errands was a mindless task!

What should have been an uneventful trip to the store completely changed my perspective on the article my friend had sent me. My friend didn't intentionally mean to hurt me. She loves me and has been my cheerleader for years. She only wanted to help me with my hair. It's time to get over my hurt, pick up my phone, and call her. I need to admit my feelings and thank her for her suggestions. Oh, and maybe make an appointment for a needed haircut!

"Bear with each other and forgive whatever grievances you may have against one another. Forgive as the Lord forgave you. And over all these virtues put on love, which binds them all together in perfect unity."

(Colossians 3:1, NIV)

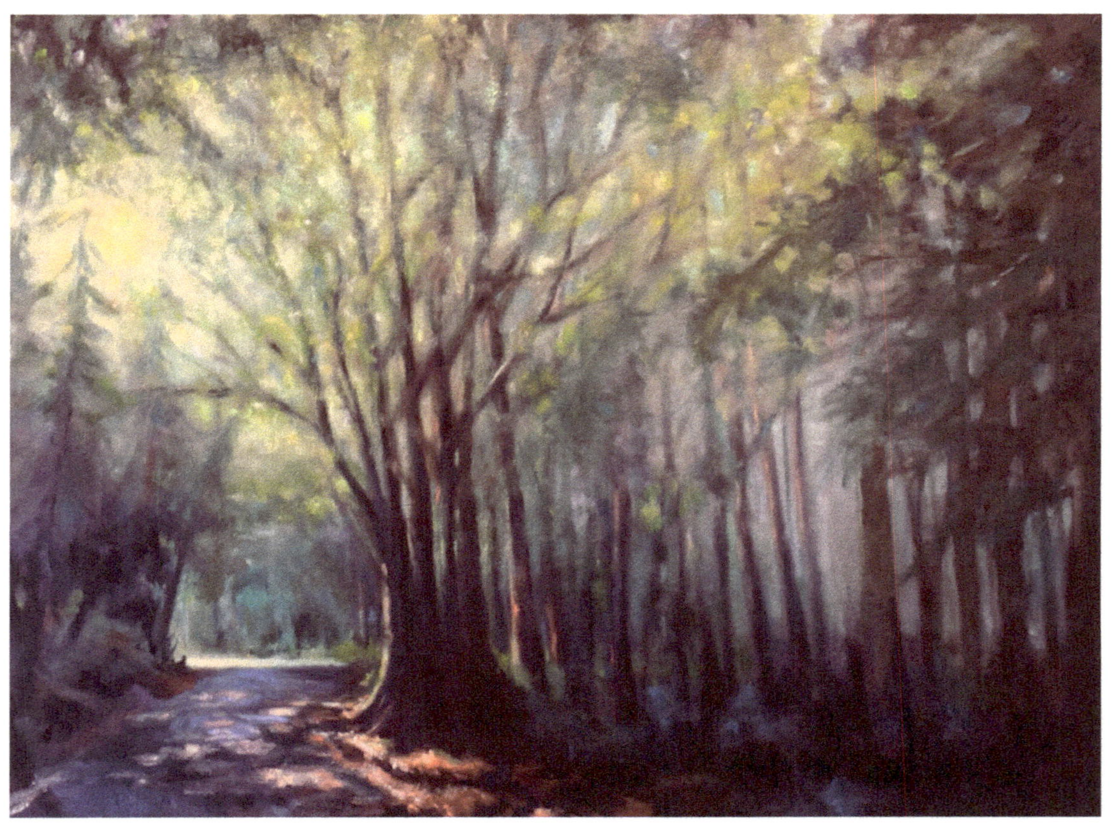

PAINTING, *HOPE AHEAD* © 2011 LEIGH D. FITZ; WRITING, 2011

Hope Ahead

Have you ever been driving and happened to see a view opening up outside your window, and you wanted to take a longer glance? It could be a sunset, a beautiful field of flowers, a glimpse of the ocean in the distance, or a tree near the side of the road dressed for a gala in fall colors.

You want to stop to capture a picture, to be a witness to beauty in nature. Your heart wants to remember this scene, to hold it close and take it with you. Maybe it brings a smile to your lips and you long to linger, letting the smile turn into laughter, but you don't stop because you "don't have time." Maybe you're in a hurry to get to wherever you're going. Maybe you feel you can't even slow down—you feel compelled to keep up with the cars speeding by around you. Perhaps you don't want to lose your place in the traffic, and even if you did have time to stop, how could you find a safe place to pull over? So, you keep your eyes on the road and move on, a discontented sigh escaping from your lips.

Sometimes, I am so focused on what's going on in front of me and the need to reach my goals, I forget to enjoy the process of my day and make a space to take pleasure in the work. Does this ever happen to you?

On the road to Salmon Beach, it's easy to stop and pull over because it's an isolated road used only by the owners and guests of the beach cabins. But for some reason, I never do, even though the view is magnificent. The mystical fog or the sunlight penetrating through the forest canopy draws me in. Yet, I don't stop, because I want to "get to the beach" where I can finally relax. I ask myself, *Is this really how I want to live my life?* I chase results and the destination instead of relishing the journey.

I look forward to events, vacations, retirement, or even the next day instead of valuing the "now." I think about what my life will be like after the next "race" is won or the next day's events are over. I want to get through the "darker" times of life quickly, as if those times will hurt less if I run past them fast enough.

But what would my life look like if I were content to lean into every moment of the day? Could gratefulness grow in the place where I am standing now? If I stop to add up all the joys and graces, naming each one—how high a number would I reach? What if I found hope on this day instead of running toward the light that tomorrow may bring or toward the next bend in the road?

My daughter, Anne, has been teaching me about this concept with her words and actions. She's making a list and keeping track of where she finds gratefulness. She stops to take pictures of beauty, gleaning stories of worth from the everyday tales of life, and creatively expands them into profound thoughts on her blog. She grabs on to opportunities where she finds joy instead of planning her life for tomorrow's benefit.

So, I stopped one day on the road to Salmon Beach, got out of my car, and took in the beauty. I then attempted to describe it with my paintbrush. The canvas I chose was three feet by four feet, large enough to capture the expanse of the forest before the bend in the road and catch the sun nearing the end of the afternoon, the time I usually arrived. I wanted to call this painting *Hope Ahead,* because of the light coming from the bend in the road, leading out of the dark forest. But Anne said, "Why not just *hope?*" because it was beautiful before the light in the distance. I think both are true—there is light in the distance and beauty I want to be grateful for in the present.

So today, I'm planning on relishing the little everyday moments and embracing each "vista," stopping to take it in and be grateful. I've noticed that it makes the journey less stressful and gives me an acute awareness of God's goodness. Stopping, appreciating, thanking, and remembering.

Now, I want to stop and see hope everywhere, not just ahead, so be careful to watch out for my brake lights!

"But those who hope in the Lord will renew their strength,
they will soar on the wings like eagles; they will run and not grow weary,
they will walk and not faint."
(Isaiah 40:31, NIV)

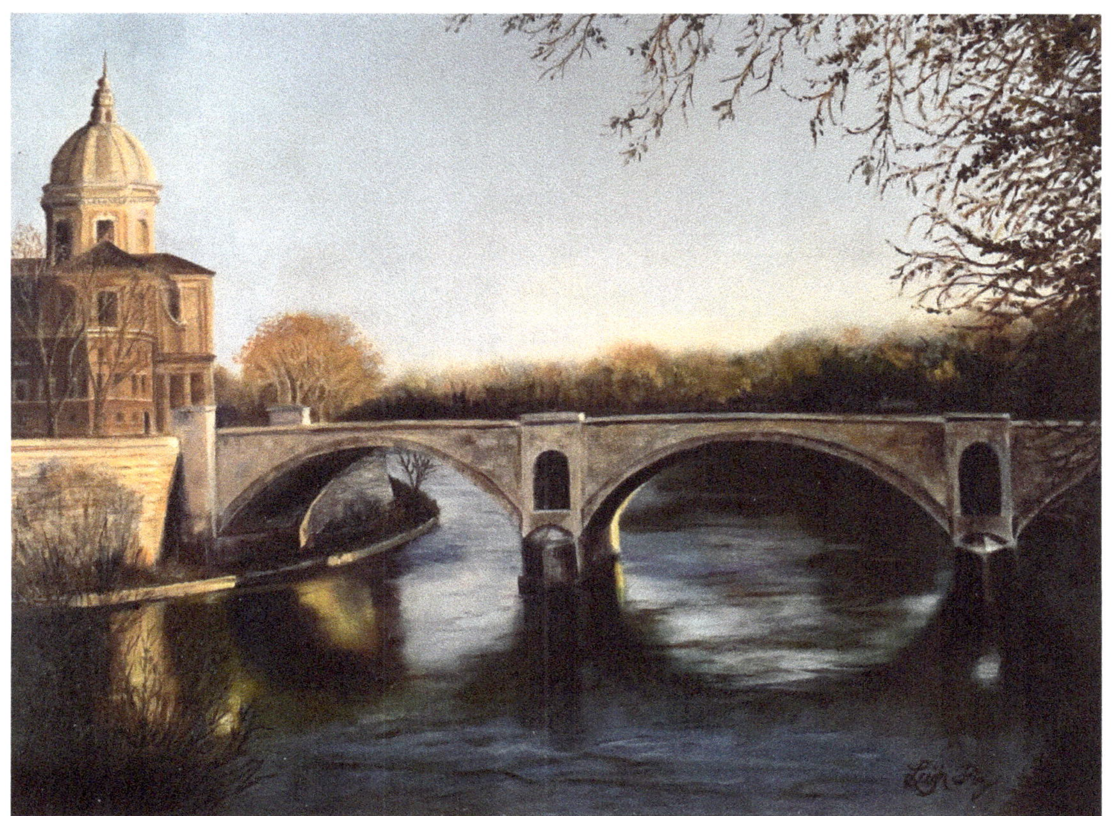

PAINTING, BRIDGEWORK © 2002 LEIGH D. FITZ; WRITING, 2003-2020

Meet Me Half-Way

This painting is of one of Rome's many bridges, and captures the light that brings life to newly budding trees, makes the buildings shine, and reflects on the Tiber River as it meanders through this ancient city. It also represents, for me, a new restoration process that took place in an old relationship—a bridge built between me and my husband, giving access and time to explore and discover new things about each other. This painting always reminds me of the bridges that connect us.

The word "bridge" conveys several meanings. As a noun, a "bridge" is a structure carrying a road, path, railroad, or canal across a river, road, or other obstacle. But as a verb, it's an act that is intended to reconcile or form a connection between two things or people.

For me, "bridging" our lives means meeting in the middle to form a connection, bringing perspective, and hopefully providing us a path to reconcile our differences—a safe crossing over the deep waters of life. We meet in the middle to keep from choosing sides, and to look with different viewpoints back toward where each of us came from, as well as forward to where we decide to go both individually, and as a couple.

I speculated there were bridges in our relationship which may have fallen into a "polite tolerance" phase of disrepair.

 In Rome, JD and I arrived on opposite sides of the river, so to speak. Our conversations had grown stale. We repeatedly talked about our kids, schedules, home repairs, money challenges, and how to juggle our busy lives, all without actually listening to or "hearing" each other. We discussed and debated the details of life, all while avoiding deeper issues, such as our communication or how the pressures at his work affected our relationship. We didn't acknowledge the feelings of resentment or sadness that were being stored rather than shared, or how we struggled to integrate back into home life at the end of the day, which sometimes felt boring in comparison to our chosen daily "work" lives.

We are two relatively different people with clashing palettes and personality profiles. JD is an intellectual; he's a physician, spreadsheet planner, extrovert, and visionary—he's spontaneous and always on the move. I, on the other hand, am an introvert who values time by myself and loves to have heartfelt conversations with family and friends. I'm an artist type, moody, easily distracted by beauty, wandering down a path of creative thought with food, flowers, plants, and oil paint as my mediums.

We were, no doubt, crazy in love with each other, but that didn't imply that we agreed with or even understood each other on every issue. We needed to actively bridge these differences, to reconcile and cultivate a path to connect back to our souls.

Rome provided this sort of "bridge" for our relationship. We determined that restoring our connection wasn't often straightforward, but it was an essential process—one that yielded profound benefits. We needed to discover strategies to intentionally meet in the middle in order to gain perspective and appreciate each other's viewpoint. Gazing at the river that flowed beneath us provided a respite, time to choose a new direction together before walking hand in hand to the other side.

This bridge also symbolizes a transition from my comfort zone to a world of new places. Italy was our first destination overseas as a couple. I was wide-eyed! I could hardly believe that I was walking down centuries-old streets and among ancient ruins. I was in a foreign country, with my husband, totally disconnected from kids, work, family, friends, and all familiar places (no cell phones at that time either!).

Being together, uninterrupted, exploring a new place, and hearing a different language spoken, was an invitation to press a "refresh" button in a relationship that had lost some of its luster, much like the marble of Rome. This place granted us the chance to relish and increase our awareness of another culture, together, while creating a sturdier bond between us. As we explored the sights, we also explored and rediscovered character qualities we were grateful for in each other, noticing joy was present as we wandered hand in hand the streets alone.

Finally, Rome reminds me to use the "bridge" as a means back to myself and to my guy. I want to remember not to let the constant details of life drown out the need for setting aside time to share our feelings and discover needed bridge repairs in our very valuable relationship.

My new message to myself and to my guy: "Meet me half way!"

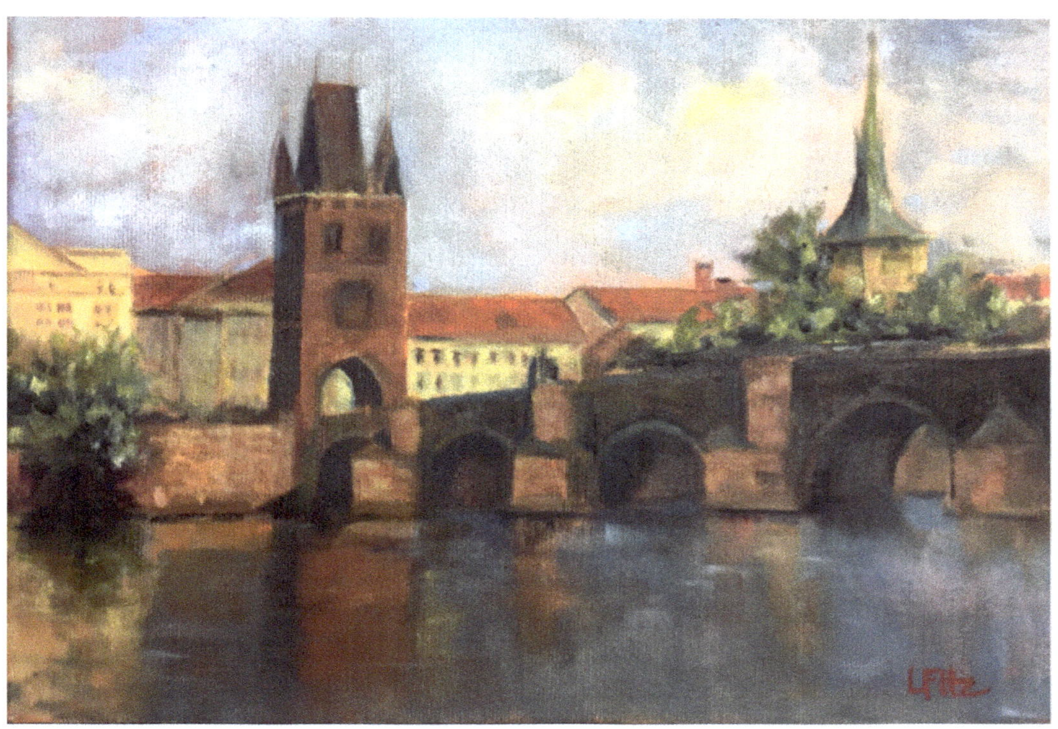

OIL PAINTING, *PRAGUE* © LEIGH D. FITZ

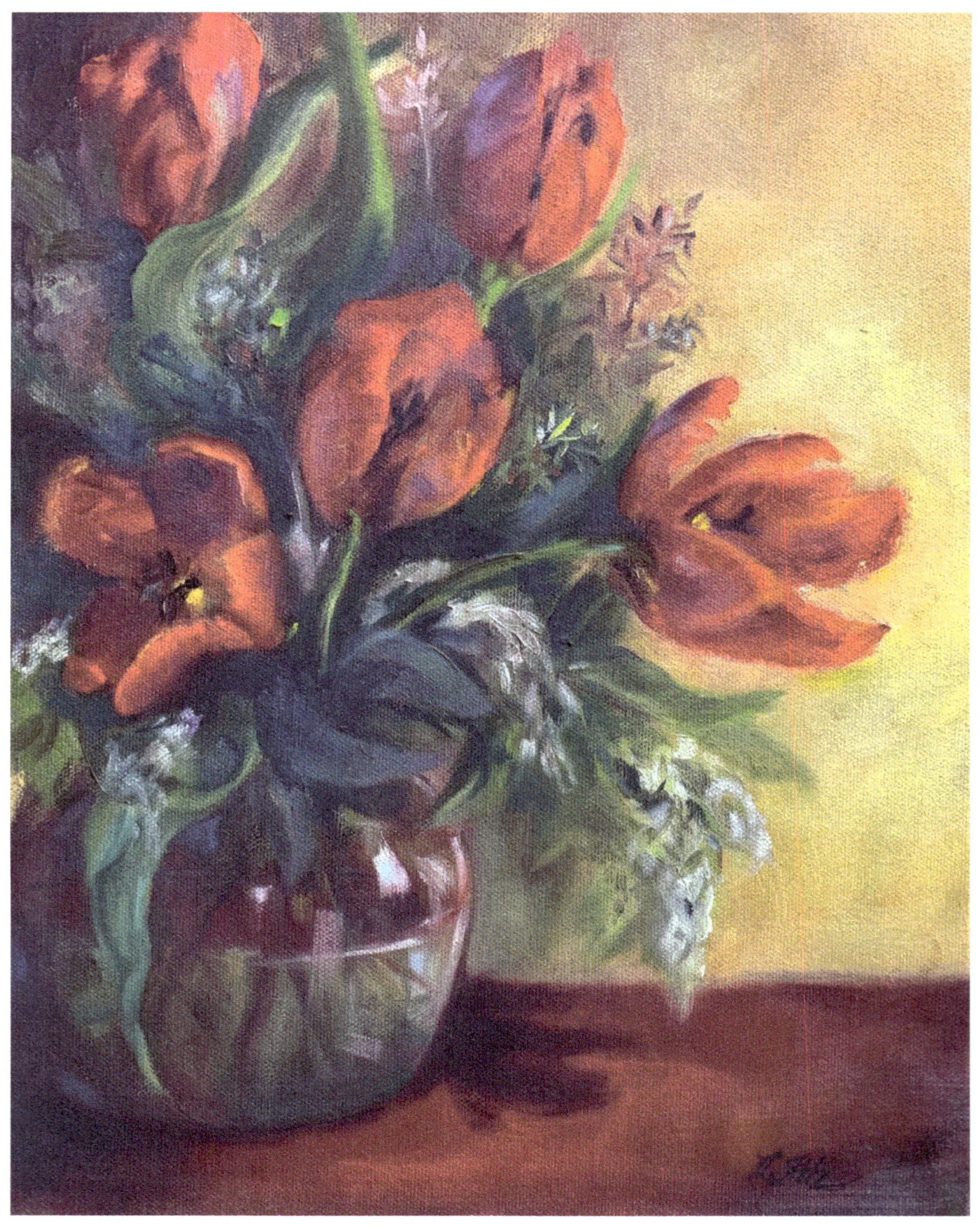

OIL PAINTING, *A JOYFUL BUNCH* © 2011 LEIGH D. FITZ; WRITING, 2011

Looking for Joy

Tulips always bring a smile to my face. They are a welcoming flower—a signal that spring has arrived. Whenever I paint them and capture their likeness on canvas, I am filled with hope and a sense of renewed joy.

Not long ago, I felt like my joy went missing. So, I set out to look for it, hoping if I found it, there would be a "filling," so to speak, of the empty places in my life. I wanted joy. I deserved joy!! I already had so much to be grateful for . . . a great husband, kids, grandkids, friends, community, a home, food, and all the basics one needs. So, where was my joy?

The dictionary defines joy as "a state of happiness or emotion of great delight caused by something exceptionally good"— but the Bible describes joy as "cheerfulness, i.e., a calm delight." Jesus said, "Remain in my love. I have told you this so that my joy may be in you, and your joy may be complete."[19]

Maybe I've been looking for joy in all the wrong places. I thought it would be helpful to remind myself to be joyful, but that turned out to be short-lived and fleeting. I thought counting my blessings would certainly do the trick and bring me joy, but again, I let the cares of life, the schedule I keep, and the aches and pains that come and go rob me of that joy.

What I've discovered is this: I can't will joy into existence or conjure it up on the spot. I can't purchase it or experience it by merely applying a smile to my face. It has to come from deep within my core so that my actions express what's already present. But how?

This morning, I read in a devotional book, "Joy is not dependent on circumstances. True joy is a byproduct of living in God's presence." This rings true to me. So, if I desire joy, I first must want God Himself. It's about remaining and abiding in Him and letting Him place His joy within me (a miraculous occurrence). Only then will my joy be complete— a calming delight!

So, if you see me with a smile on my face, a twinkle in my eyes, and a bit of joyous laughter erupting from within me, chances are it's because earlier in my day I sat as close to Jesus as I could so that He could place His joy in me. However, I'm finding it's not a one-time event. I can't get joy today once and for all. No, it takes

19. John 15:11, NIV

abiding and "hanging out" with God. Joy simply comes from God, and so I am deciding to stay connected each and every day.

After all my searching, it turns out the dictionary was right! "Joy is a state of happiness, or an emotion of great delight caused by something exceptionally good," except it failed to mention that the "something exceptionally good" is God!

I've stopped looking for joy now because I know where to find it. Instead, I'm trying to figure out how to abide with God daily and let Him abide in me. Like tulips, that always brings me joy!

*"You make known to me the path of life; you fill me with joy in your presence,
with eternal pleasures at your right hand."*
(Psalm 16:11, NIV)

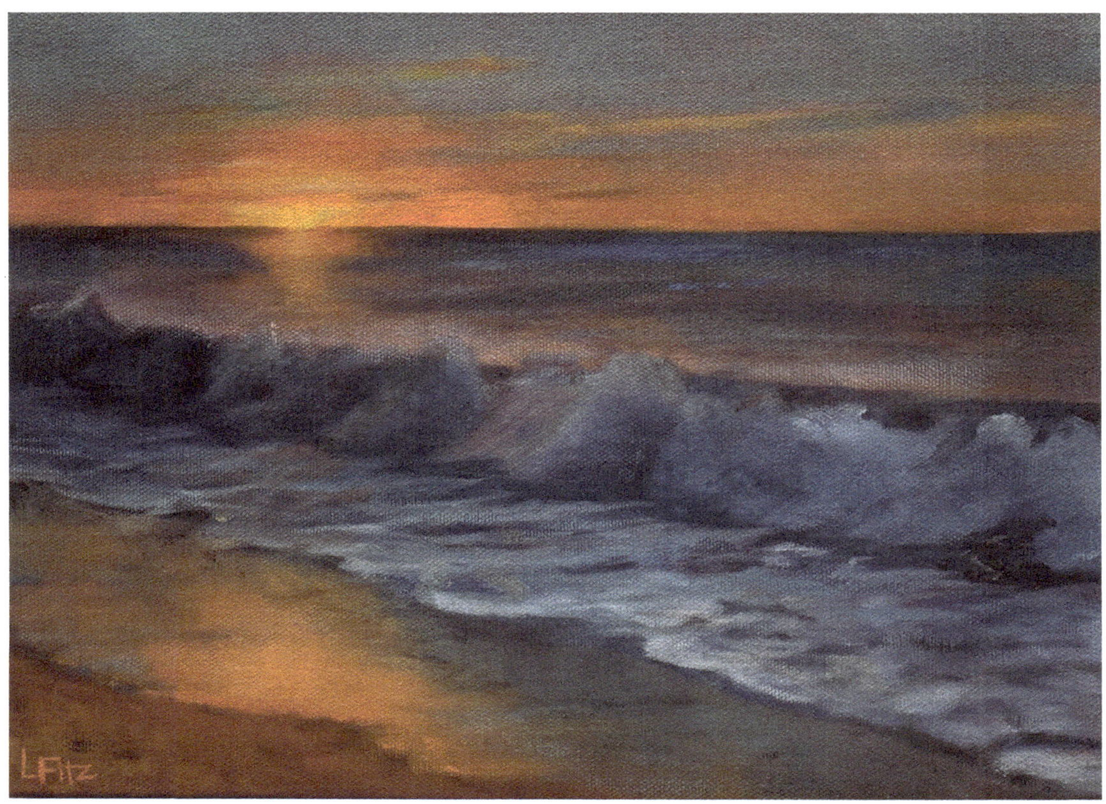

OIL PAINTING, *WAKING UP ON TIME* © 2019 LEIGH D. FITZ, 2019 (SUNRISE OVER THE SEA OF CORTEZ); JOURNAL ENTRY, 2009

Wake up and Live Your Dreams

I had a dream last night that seemed worthy enough to record and ponder:

A woman sought the assistance of an interior designer to formulate a design for a gathering place in her home. After hours of planning, looking for the perfect furniture, and gathering samples of fabric and paint, the designer put together an intricate model in a small box. It represented the finished room with color, textiles, furniture, drapes, rugs, art, and everything needed to complete the room in style. She presented the box to her client, who loved it and didn't want to change a thing—but she also wanted to ask her friends for their feedback before moving ahead.

The woman took the little model to show to her friends and family and see what they would say. She displayed the model in her home to show her guests whenever they stopped by. Everyone seemed to love the idea! She had the money to buy all that was needed to bring her dream to fruition, and she had all the various skilled people to do the work. She even had a contractor to orchestrate the timeline and take care of every last detail. She had all the components to create a beautiful room, except, seemingly, the confidence to say the simple words, "Yes, let's do it!"

For some reason, doubt had crept in. *Would it be the most beautiful room possible? Would everybody love it? Is there anything better?*

The woman carried around the little model wherever she went, longing for reassurance, but her friends were tired of discussing the topic and started avoiding her. The model began to show signs of wear and eventually started to fall apart. She lost the names and numbers of workers; there were pieces of furniture that became unavailable and her contractor grew tired of waiting and took other jobs. What had started as a plan of great potential ended up a mere dream of what could have been.

What does my dream mean? Maybe it means something different to everyone reading this. I see myself in the various characters, but especially the main character. This woman had tremendous opportunity to change the future, but lacked the confidence to follow through with the ideas. She held tightly to her doubts. She lacked the courage to overcome the fear of potential failure, as judged by her friends to whom she gave the power to be the judge and jury of her work. Thus, her energy and passion were depleted and she was stalled.

There are other possible interpretations. Others of us grow weary from trying to help these "characters" in our lives, perhaps getting frustrated that our advice isn't appreciated. Or, like the designer who had great ideas and artful taste, we can't implement our designs without the go ahead from some other person.

What could have been? The woman could have said, "Yes!" A room could have been created—a space made to welcome others into and be nourished by friendship. A designer's confidence could have been boosted with potential future clients forthcoming. Workers could have been paid for their skill and had the ability to put food on the table for their families. What else? Goodness, love, joy, peace, contentment—all delivered from this one woman's dream.

Wake up! There is still time. I believe that God, in His grace and power, gives us second chances. Wake up from slumber. All is not lost! God is gently shaking me from my sleep, saying, "Wake up, wash the sleep from your crusted eyes, and see Me at work in you." Get up, begin again, it's not too late to recover the dreams dreamt yesterday.

Post Script:

This was written in my journal in 2012. My "dream" (for over ten years, as of this writing) was to create a book filled with my paintings and writings, but my doubts held me securely from moving toward that dream. Fear of failure is something I battle with daily. Both God and my husband kept shaking me awake to tell me it wasn't too late to start. I'm grateful that I finally stopped dreaming and got to work.

I chose this particular painting to illustrate this chapter, a sunrise over the Sea of Cortez in Baja. When we were there in March of last year, we had to set our alarms for 5:30 a.m. every day in order to grab a cup coffee and watch the sunrise on the beach. I missed a couple of mornings because I couldn't wake up. I wanted to sleep. Each morning the sunrise was distinctly different, so it was a disappointment to miss even one.

"He who began a good work in you will carry it on to completion
until the day of Christ Jesus."
(Philippians 1:6, NIV)

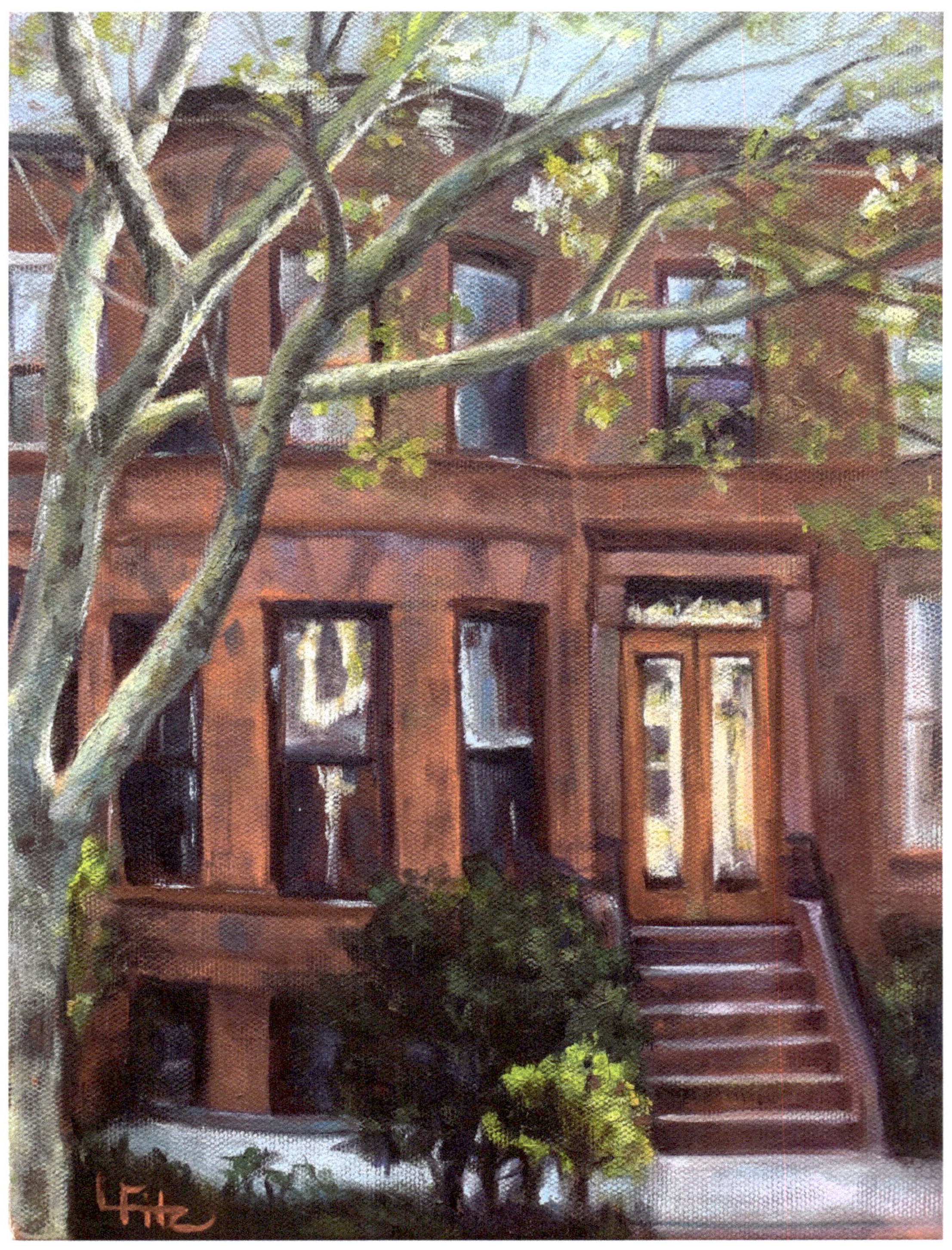

OIL PAINTING, *BROOKLYN* © 2015 LEIGH D. FITZ; WRITING, 2020

Beginning in Brooklyn

My great-grandfather became a US citizen in 1883 and resided in Brooklyn, where my grandparents met, fell in love, married, and raised their children. I, too, was born in a Brooklyn hospital but raised on Long Island, NY. This painting of a Brooklyn Brownstone depicts the home where my dad lived during his boyhood. It reminds me of my roots and my love for my parents. It evokes gratefulness for those that came before me and the rich heritage I've been given.

As I painted it, I re-explored my memories of my dad. My relationship with him was complicated in the beginning. I was terrified of him while growing up because he had an anger management problem. But of course, I didn't realize *he* had a problem; I thought maybe it was me.

I never knew when he would explode, and when he did, it was scary and chaotic.

I can still remember the fear in my mother's face. I would freeze, too scared to move. If his anger was aimed at me, he would point his finger, coming slowly toward me, yelling. He would sometimes grab me by the collar, lifting me closer to his face and to his harsh words. I was spanked for an array of childish behaviors, like for leaving my chewing gum on the corner of the buffet in our dining room. (I needed a place to stow it while I was eating, of course.) I'm guessing I was five at the time.

I recall another time being punished for tipping over some signs he had made for a church event that, in my defense, were leaning precariously against the wall in our kitchen. I happened to accidentally brush against one, sending the rest cascading like dominoes to the floor. My dad erupted and told me to go up to my room and lean over the bed. He took out his frustrations on me with a T-ruler, but what hurt the most were the blows inflicted on my heart. I was twelve at the time, and well on my way into womanhood, so lowering my pants to his ruler caused me severe embarrassment and humiliation.

I think he, too, realized that I was too old to spank, for he never did it again. I would like to believe that he offered forgiveness, hugs, or reassurance of his love after his outbursts, but I don't remember such offerings. My mom would remind me that he loved me now and then, but I needed to hear him speak the words. Unfortunately, his discipline and anger stood alone, and consequently I felt unlovable.

Some memories can be so enormous and emotionally charged or damaging that there's little space in my mind to fit in the moments of goodness which I can only believe existed. But as I painted this home and reflected on my father's entire life, willing my mind to remember the good things he did in those days, they began to seep back into my memory.

In elementary school, he told me I was the best "pot scrubber" in the family. This was one of the only times I can remember that he complimented me, so I held tightly to this one (and still keep my pots scrubbed today!).

I can still hear him descending the squeaky stairs of our house in Michigan early in the morning before anyone else was up in order to read his Bible and spend time alone with God. I noticed he was so faithfully dedicated to this practice that I started to make my own attempt to read my Bible. I also noticed that when he returned to wake us up, he was always whistling.

He read the Bible to us every morning after breakfast, and we each prayed before we left for school. We were a family that ate breakfast and dinner together every morning and night and often stayed around the table to talk. Those were good times. I learned the importance of family dinners from my mom and dad. We played ping pong in the basement of our home. He loved to tell jokes, pull pranks, and planned elaborate parties for us kids.

As my parents turned forty, they felt compelled to sell their lovely home in Michigan and move us to California, so my dad could attend Fuller Theological Seminary, thinking he would become a pastor. He gave up his engineering career, and their friends, and sold their five-bedroom, five-bath home along with practically everything in it. They moved us into a two-bedroom, one-bath bungalow (I'm guessing it was around 1,200 square feet) in Pasadena.

I remember being amazed by my parents' ability to give away so many things out of their deep love for God. I recognized that they loved God more than their antiques or spacious house. I never heard any complaints from my mother. (I thought about this move often, especially when I turned forty and was living in my own sizable home.) At the time of the move, I was entering seventh grade, and my sisters were in ninth and eleventh. The three of us shared an eight-foot by ten-foot bedroom with one bunk bed and a rollaway bed under the bottom bunk. (I also noticed arguments diminished compared to when we each had a room of our own.) My dad brilliantly made an L-shaped wall desk and divided it into three sections. We each had counter space, a drawer, and a wall mirror with bookshelves above the mirrors, to give each of us a place to study at night and a place to fix our hair and makeup in the mornings. Soon after we moved to California, my mom got pregnant and gave birth to my brother, bringing a whole new dimension to our family—a seventeen-year span between the first and the last.

After graduating from seminary, my dad started working for World Vision and later became one of the vice presidents, a position he would hold for the next twenty-five years. During this time, he was constantly thinking, traveling, and strategizing on how to effectively spread the good news of the gospel. He researched and documented the "unreached groups" around the world who had never heard of the love of Jesus. He authored a variety of books on faith, planning, and strategizing for life, leadership, and God. His life verse described him well: "A man plans his ways but the LORD determines his steps."[20]

Dad continued his practice of getting up early to spend time with God. The California house was so small, however, that I could hear the sound of him turning on the light next to the couch in the living room. As I grew older, I could see the effects, firsthand, this practice had on my dad's heart, developing him into a man full of integrity and wisdom. He lost his temper less often. He told me that he started to pen his prayers in a journal to keep him focused and remember answered prayers. In high school, I started hunting around for blank books, which were scarce in those days, to give to him as gifts. By college, I was penning my prayers in blank books as well. This, too, was a gift he gave to me. He took the time to answer my questions about God, theology, or verses in the Bible I was struggling over.

I see bits and pieces of myself in him. As an aeronautical engineer, he designed and patented flight instruments. With a little research, I found some of his designs and drawings—pieces of artwork. One summer, he started carving a fish from a block of wood. As he carved, he would say, "There's a fish in here that's trying to get out!" He continued to whittle various things over the years, hanging them in his home. I remember my first Christmas away from my parents, married, three thousand miles away in a new state (Maryland), feeling alone. As a Christmas gift, my dad sent me one of his carvings. It meant the world to me that he gave me something *he* had created. I remember how loved I felt by him *for the first time in my life*. I was twenty-four years old.

My most cherished memories of my dad are the last few years of his life. Long-distance phone calls and travel back and forth between Washington State and Southern California to see both my parents brought us closer than ever. He started corresponding with me regularly through emails, confiding in me his concerns for my mom as she entered the world of Alzheimers. As the years progressed, it was frightening and so difficult for us to watch this woman we loved and adored slowly slip away.

After she died, he and I communicated almost daily as he grieved and sorted through all he was thinking and feeling. He came to see me and stayed at our little beach cabin, where we sat most afternoons, talking for hours. It was here, at the end of his life, that I knew him best and discovered his tenderness and his love for me. Almost a year after my mom died, he called me one night and asked if I could fly down to see him. I said, "I'd love to; when do you want me to come, Dad?"

He responded, "How about tomorrow?" My heart sank, for my schedule was busy, and one of my kids was in a bit of a crisis. I told him I couldn't come that quickly, but I would buy a ticket for the following week.

20. Proverbs 16:9

He must have sensed that his death was imminent, for he died a couple of hours after I arrived. Do I wish I had dropped everything and flown down to California to see him? Yes, but I have to believe I made the best choice considering the circumstances; I don't feel any regret because there was nothing left "unsaid" between us. Losing both my parents within a year felt like a piece of my heart was forever ripped away. I cherish their memory.

As I look at this painting again, I am reminded of all the good memories with my dad, creating space for love, kindness, and forgiveness to fill my mind, squeezing out any hurtful thoughts left lingering. He was not a perfect man nor a perfect father, but as my dad, Edward Dayton was quite remarkable. The following quote describes him well.

"Do all the good you can
In all the ways you can
In all the places you can
At all the times you can
To all the people you can
As long as ever you can."
—John Wesley

My dad modeled faith in God for me. He led a life of goodness and mercy. He taught me the worth of doing a job well, like scrubbing pots until they shine.

Help When Helpless

Diagnosing and treating my breast cancer this year required me to see three oncologists, and undergo a myriad of tests and treatments to prevent cancer from returning: mammograms, ultrasounds, lab work, a biopsy, surgery, pathology, lymph node harvesting, radiation therapy, and drug therapy. On top of all that, there was the healing of the wounds those treatments incurred. As I look back on it all, I realize I was so focused on my treatment for cancer that I missed the tumors of selfishness, joylessness, pride, and complacency that, too, were growing.

When it comes to the physical demise of the body, there are physicians to help. But, who helps heal the heart from sadness? Who can see into the soul of a person to apply a salve that comforts the wounds of worry? Who knows the thoughts of human beings and understands the complexity of our personalities. Who can treat selfishness and pride?

Who knows how to grow gratefulness and joy in a heart full of restlessness? What surgeon can see and re-move the disease of complacency and self-absorption that can set me on a path toward emotional imbalance? In my experience, only God can. If cancer hadn't been discovered in my body, I might have never caught a glimpse of these unhealthy attitudes in my life.

Caring for one's heart, mind, and soul plays a considerable part in the process of becoming well. The body may continue on a downward course, even with the best of care. This is, after all, the cycle of life. Yet, in these arduous circumstances, I sometimes felt isolated in my fears and doubts. What was most helpful for me during that time were other people's expressions of sorrow, sympathy, and love. It was beneficial to be asked how I was coping or feeling. I felt cherished by those that cried with me unashamedly.

Curiosity, I found, did not serve me well when I first was given a cancer diagnosis. I could only absorb so much information at a time. Initially, hearing the words, "You have cancer," was enough to sit with for awhile.

Prayers directed at the disease, I felt, were essential for me, but I needed prayer for peace of mind, free-dom from fear and anxiety, and so much more. When friends asked me what they could do, my response was, "Pray for peace!" (And I didn't mean world peace.)

My emotions were raw—continually trembling. I needed courage to step into this "valley of shadows and death," and I needed to know I wasn't alone in the journey. A cancer diagnosis was never going to be a get-well-in-a-week sort of prayer. I needed prayer over the months of care and recovery, which, of course, takes devotion on the part of other people. I am a person who believes in the power of prayer, but to be honest, I found it more challenging to pray for myself in those months. I lacked strength. Exhaustion lived with me full time.

My family and friends did such a great job of encouraging me with kind words and love through text messages and phone calls. I'm guessing we all multitask when we're on the phone, but during that time of my life, I was grateful when the person on the other end seemed "all in."

One morning, our daughter, Anne, called me as she was washing breakfast dishes. She was still when she sensed I needed to talk; she stopped and listened intently over the next couple of hours as I wept and spoke for the first time since my diagnosis about my deep fear and anxiety, wondering out loud how this was going to affect my life. It was an enormous gift of both time and love to me personally.

One night, JD and I watched the movie *The Notebook*—a couple's love story that ends in the death of the woman when she is in her late sixties. Sad, yes, but it afforded us a moment to unleash our sorrow to grieve. We were both in tears, but as the credits rolled, we held each other and sobbed uncontrollably, wondering out loud how this great love of ours would eventually come to an end.

The next morning, in my journal, I wrote, "I'm already missing him even though we haven't parted, even though neither of us has taken our last breath. I'm overwhelmed with the thought that one day in the future, one of us will die first. Maybe getting cancer gives me that realization that we are in our last years. I don't care about what age I am when I die; I just don't want to face life with only half of me—without him—nor do I want him to be alone." That tender moment re-established in me the desire to make every day of our married life count for good, and keep looking for ways to cultivate our love.

Interestingly, I kept two journals in the first year after diagnosis. One recorded my thoughts, my grief, my pain, and the other documented everything I could think of that I was grateful for. Gratefulness kept me focused.

The first thing I did every morning was to write in this journal. It redirected my thoughts, causing my eyes to be on the lookout for goodness and grace to show up (even if it was just the first ray of light on the bare trees behind my house, the taste of coffee on my lips, or the hummingbird visiting the feeder outside my window). As my list grew in numbers, so did my joy. It was a mind shift. I sensed a glimmer of hope or a bit of joy rise in my soul, healing my inner self. Joy shows its face only if I'm willing to open my eyes and acknowledge its presence.

At the six-month mark, my gratitude journal held over one thousand entries with two hundred and ten directly related to cancer. This felt key, balancing gratefulness with grief. My niece Jessica wrote similar thoughts on her Facebook page as she sorted out her own "fresh wound" of loss. She said, "Sadness is okay. Letting the pain out is healing. But I'm learning that I don't have to live in one camp or the other. Just because you're grieving something doesn't mean you can't be full of joy. And being thankful and focused on what you do have doesn't mean you're just putting on a good face and forcing yourself to be happy. I want my sad feelings to have a voice, to be processed, to be heard (by God and others), to allow God and others to hold me in those deep places of pain. But I don't want to live there. That's not where life continues—and I refuse to let sorrow steal from me or tell me who my God is."

I, too, needed to permit myself to step away from the whole subject of cancer and my loss. I needed a break from the sadness. Writing in my gratitude journal each day gave me such a break. And for me, it was more than just naming each item I was grateful for; it was writing my thanks to God for all the good that my senses discovered.

Disruptive grace. It's been a whirlwind—scary, inconvenient, painful, tiring, worrisome, tear-filled, humbling—a full spectrum of emotions, tumbled together into craziness and disorder. But grace was there too. Grace came to me in the form of family and friends, neighbors, those that administered love with words, flowers, food, cards, text messages, and cookies. Grace arrived in the disguise of sweet-smelling hand cream, phone calls just to say "hi," visitors bearing gifts of brownies, chocolates, wine, candles, a cozy quilt, or a smile. I felt loved, which, in my mind, was THE best medicine, bringing joy to my heart and speeding up my physical healing.

The most significant form of grace came to me through my husband's tenderness. He sat with me in pain, wept with me, reached for me, or rubbed my back during my sleepless nights, whispering words of love. He prayed for me, left cute notes for my finding, took care of the house, and listened to my endless stream of consciousness and questions. We laughed as well, with our inside jokes, banter, and teasing. He refused to let cancer take away our silliness or happiness.

I will relish the memories of God's presence and His love. In those moments alone, still shocked and overwhelmed that any of this could be happening to me, He kept calming me through Scripture. I had the sense that all these disruptions, as uncomfortable as they seemed, were worth the knowing, really knowing that God was and is right with me, administering His grace like water—spreading to all the nooks and crannies of my body in excess. It is more than sufficient. The unexplainable peace that God Himself, and the prayers of others, carried me. Even knowing the story isn't over (I'm still part of this cancer club that I had not wished to join), grace remains.

So, I'm clinging to both JD and God. I'm clinging because I don't want to lose this sense of closeness and peace as I get well. Statistics are in my favor, yet I don't want to lose my resolve to live each day fully. It's a great gift to have this new excitement bubbling up in me to live each day well with no regrets. But having said that, I still have to live just one day at a time, sorting through my thoughts and emotions. Seemingly without any notice, doubt arrives, yanking on my sleeve, pulling me away from peace into a web of despair.

I still start my day (nearly three years later), writing in a gratitude journal because I don't want to forget these months of treatment, not only for my cancer but for my soul as well. Years from now, I want to reread what life was like during these months, and remember how God and all the people in my life collaboratively held my hand and my heart, changing sorrow into laughter. I am grateful, truly grateful.

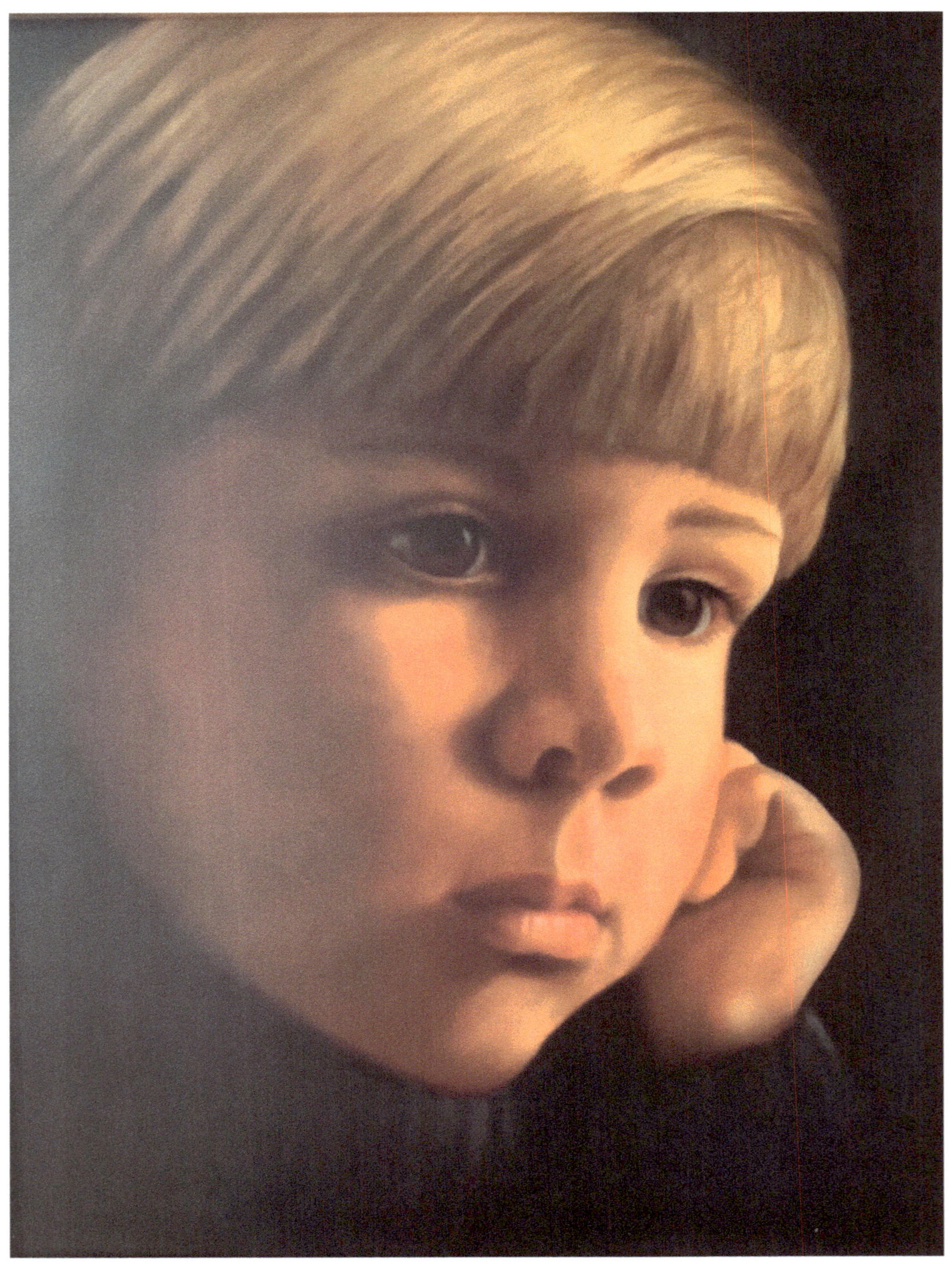

PAINTING, *MY SON* © 2003 LEIGH D. FITZ; WRITING, 2009

Mother's Day

Mother's Day always makes me smile, whether I think back to the mother I had, to the mother I am, or to my daughters amid their own motherhood. Indeed, to birth a baby that is a part of your flesh is an experience that never leaves you. The first time that little one intently looks into your eyes and then gives you a big smile, your heart melts and is given to them forever.

Having a baby placed in your arms, by his mother, as a gift, is an extraordinary miracle, as well. You protect your heart at first, wondering if she will change her mind, but then, despite the uncertainty, you fall hopelessly in love with that little one. You become his mother, and he becomes your child. At least, this was my experience. My first daughter arrived through my birth canal, my second was lifted from my womb in an emergency C-section, and my third was placed in my arms, just over my heart, through adoption. Miracle babies given three different ways, yet all mine—making me a mother of three.

I always pictured myself with a boatload of kids. I wanted to be a mother, but first things first. Having a house, money in savings, secure jobs, all of that needed to come first—maybe in my thirties would be the time for mothering to begin.

JD and I talked about wanting at least four kids: birthing two, and then perhaps adopting a couple more. But when I was twenty-four, two years into our marriage, I sought medical help because of a growing internal pain near my uterus. After the examination, my doctor told me to make another appointment, but the next time, to bring my husband, and he would tell me then what was wrong with me. *(Can you imagine?!)*

I freaked out and said I wasn't leaving until he informed me. He told me I had endometriosis, and that he would discuss it further when I brought my husband back. JD was in medical school at the time, so I frantically went to find him to tell him what I had, or rather to ask what on earth I had, and what did this mean!? I thought, admittedly, I was dying of some horrible disease.

At the next visit, the doctor told us that my endometriosis (a condition resulting from the appearance of endometrial tissue outside the uterus and causing pelvic pain) would only get worse with time and would eventually cause me to be infertile. We were told, "If you want children, you need to start trying as soon as possible."

The thought of not having a child devastated us, so we didn't hesitate. This news came just a couple of weeks before we were to move from our small flat in San Francisco to Maryland, where JD would begin his internship and residency at Walter Reed Hospital in Washington, DC. The doctor also told me that all these life changes associated with the move—camping across the country and starting my new job—would likely keep me from conceiving right away, so to be patient. We began to pray for a little one.

Our first daughter, Anne, was born nine months later! So much for worrying! I loved being pregnant, and I loved having a daughter even more. Anne filled our home with joy and gratitude.

She was an easy baby, loving to be held, and I had all the time in the world to do just that. Soon after Anne turned one, I wanted to try to get pregnant again. Nine months later, our adorable Kate was born. She had a mind of her own and didn't want to be contained by my arms, and once she could crawl she got extremely creative. Kate had an imaginary friend named Amy and would give us daily reports about Amy and her parents, Tom and Maureen. She sang songs she made up on the fly about life and kept us in stitches at the dinner table. She brought laughter and wonderment to our home.

Our girls were ages three and five when we moved to Washington State with the military, to Madigan Army Hospital. By then my desire for more children crept back into my thinking, but my endometriosis had returned with a vengeance and my pain started increasing from a few days to whole weeks each month. The only way to heal was a complete hysterectomy, which I had at age thirty-two.

We wanted to adopt, but because we had close friends who were applying to adopt, I didn't dare hope for more children for myself. A few months before my thirty-fifth birthday, my friend Trina told me she felt an impression that I would have a son. I actually laughed at her words, and informed her that, due to the hysterectomy, it was a total impossibility. Her response was a direct quote from Scripture, "Nothing is impossible with God!"

A few months later, an elderly woman from church, whom my girls and I had befriended, also informed me that God had told her He was giving us a son. Again, I discounted it as "impossible." Two weeks later, I received a call from an attorney's wife who asked me if I would be open to adopting a baby that was about to be born. The mother had rejected all of the resumes of potential adoptive parents because she had insisted that the parents had to already have kids so that her child would have siblings.

We jumped at the chance and sent in a resume. Weeks later, a precious teenage girl placed our miracle bundle, Michael, in my arms, saying, with tears rolling down her cheeks, "You are everything I hope to be one day, but I'm not now, and I want my son to have the best." She also told us that when she held our application in her hands (before she read it), she felt God's hands on her shoulders and His voice in her ear, saying, "This is the family I have chosen for your son." With our new son, Michael, we felt our family was complete.

This portrait is of Michael when he was about five years old, and it was the first portrait I ever attempted. I was thrilled to see his eyes appear on the canvas and witness his likeness looking back at me. He had, and still does have, a great smile, but honestly, I didn't want to attempt painting teeth, and so I settled for this picture that I had of him with his little hand tucked under his chin, looking introspective. I always wondered what he was thinking about. He was one of those kids whom you always knew was thinking deeply about life, and his comments were full of wisdom even at an early age. He brought a huge amount of love and a spirit of kindness to our home.

I love being a mom to these three kids! One of my favorite memories was the nightly routine of putting them to bed and making my rounds to tuck them in and listen to their prayers. Each would request a song for me to sing, and a back rub. They always seemed to be more talkative at bedtime, and willing to speak of their struggles or fears. Even as teenagers, they still asked me to "come to say goodnight."

My parenting years are long ago ended and my kids have morphed into becoming my friends, but I will always, always be their mom — who profoundly loves each of them dearly.

"I prayed for this child, and the LORD has granted me what I asked of Him."
(1 Samuel 1:27, NIV)

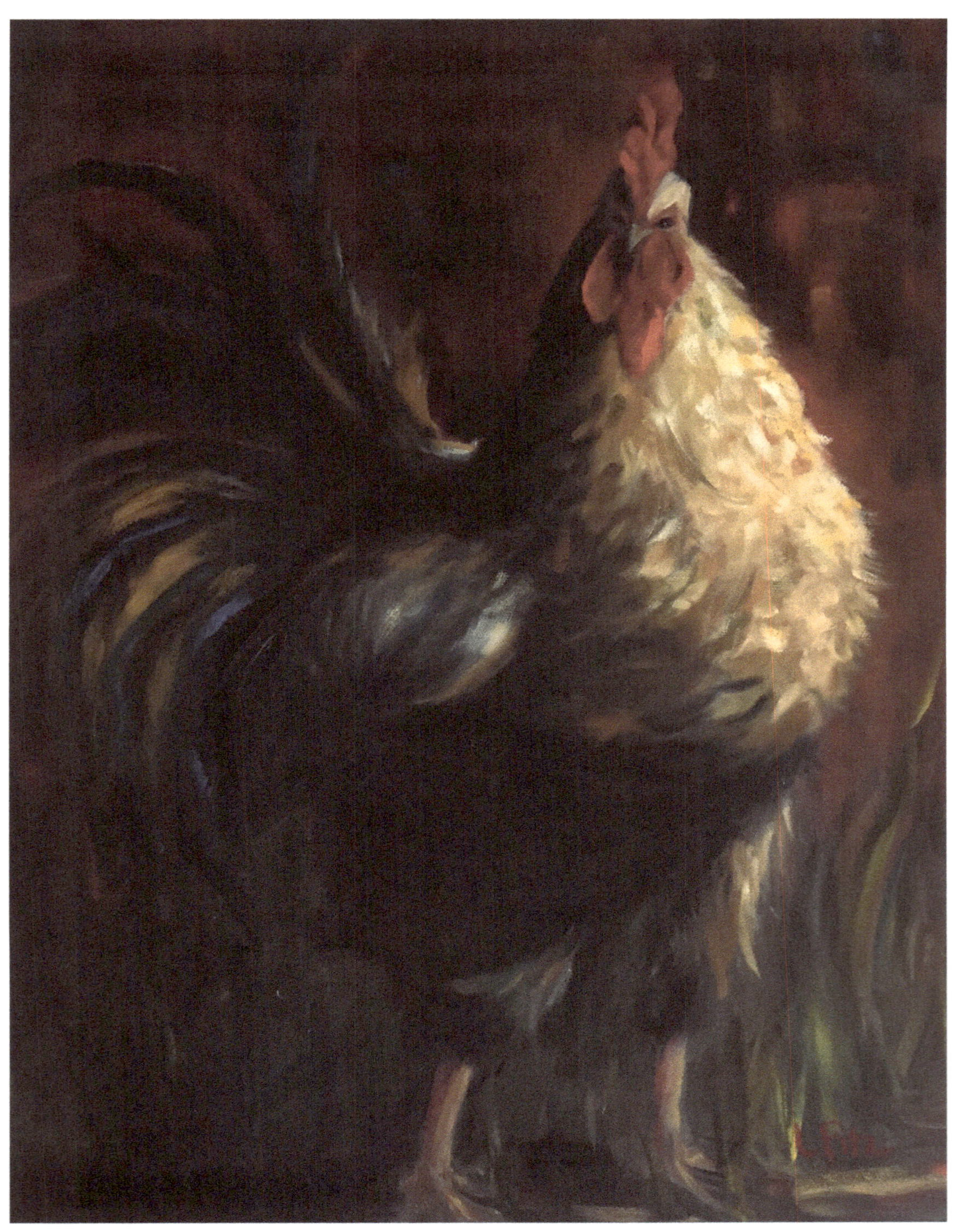

OIL PAINTING, *BEFORE THE ROOSTER CROWS* © 2008 LEIGH D. FITZ; WRITING, 2010

Before the Cock Crows

This painting reminds me of myself—how I can so easily become puffed up with pride or get my "feathers ruffled" by others. This bird stands with attitude, ready for a fight. He is turned from the light almost defiantly.

This painting also reminds me to keep short accounts with those close to me, and with my God, as it reminds me of the rooster crowing just after Peter denied Christ. It raises the question of whether I am somehow denying that I know Christ through my words or actions. It asks me: is the rooster crowing to remind me to keep short accounts and admit my wrongdoing to God and the people I love?

I once led my church in a community prayer of confession that I still find relevant for myself today:

"Father God, I thank You and praise You that You have the power to forgive sin. We come to You this morning with clean clothes, showered, and our hair combed, yet some of us remain a dirty mess on the inside because of sin in our lives. I believe You will forgive us if we are willing to confess and admit where we failed to obey. When Peter realized the rooster was crowing and remembered that Jesus had predicted he would deny Him three times before the cock crowed, he "broke down and wept bitterly."[21] *I wonder if he wept in front of everyone. I ask myself why my eyes are usually dry when I realize I've sinned. I attempt to cut myself a break, thinking, 'Surely, I am not as bad as others.'*

Forgive me, Lord. Forgive my pride, my cover-ups, and my lack of tears. Forgive me for seeing the needs of others this week but not responding because I had my own schedule to keep. Father, forgive me for bringing the same sins over and over again to You, as if forgiveness were cheap. But it wasn't. You paid for it with your Son's life. I'm sorry, Father. I'm asking You, as each one of us prays silently before You this morning, that You will hear us and forgive, and pour Your Holy Spirit on us in a fresh way that causes conviction, repentance, and a restored heart of joy."

It's helpful for me to have reminders in life that point me in the right direction and toward the need to fess up to my mistakes, seeking forgiveness from those I hurt. This feathered friend assists me with this process, although I often wish he'd tone down the volume of his screech and the frequency of his squawking!

"If we confess our sin he is able and just to forgive us our sins
and cleanse us from all unrighteousness."
(1 John 1:9, NIV)

21. Luke 22:62

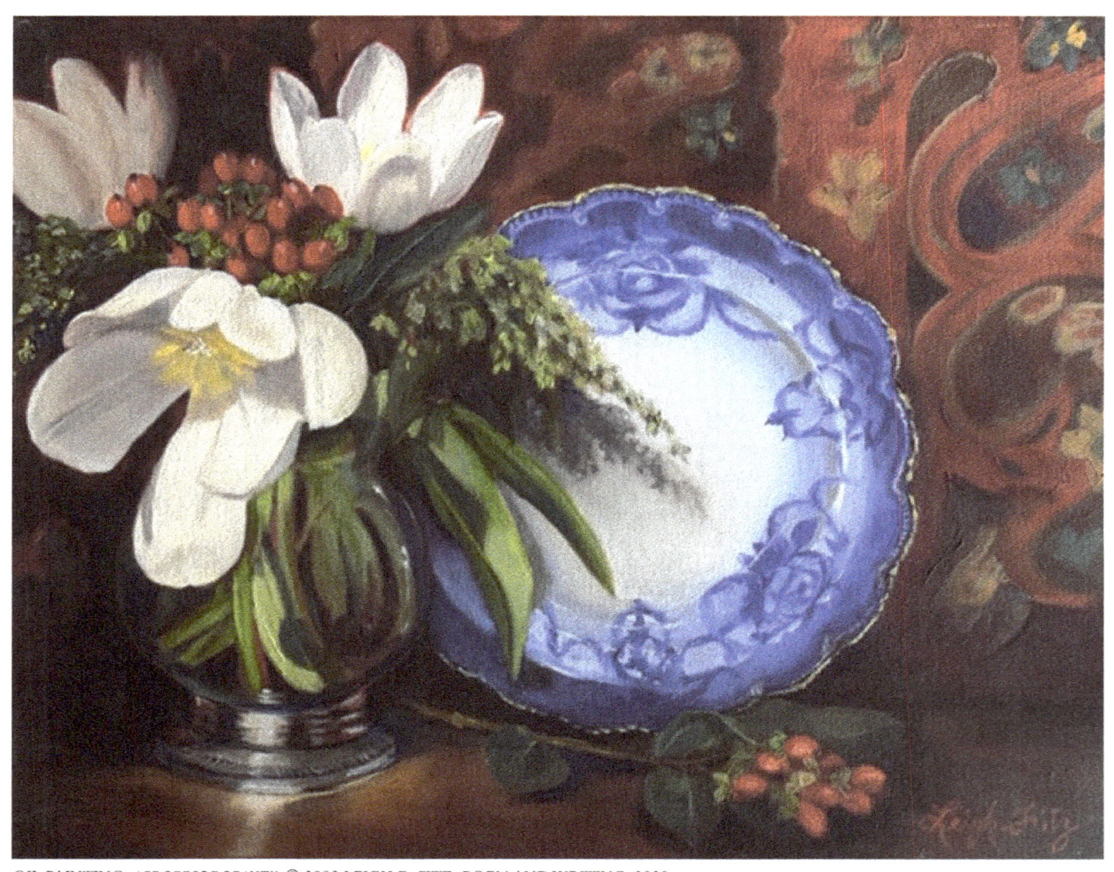

OIL PAINTING, *AGE BEFORE BEAUTY* © 2003 LEIGH D. FITZ; POEM AND WRITING, 2020

Age before Beauty

Outer Beauty wins admiration but rarely a friend.
She turns a head, but not a heart.
Gathering compliments, but no sweet words of love.
She refuses to be held,
Slipping away like water between my tightened fingers.

Outer Beauty began packing at fifty,
No matter that I begged her to stay.
As I apply makeup to hide her departure,
My heart feels further hidden.

Choosing Inner Beauty,
I hand my paintbrush to God.
He paints mercy and kindness.
And, as my inner peace swells,
My worry lines fill.

Like the tulip, true beauty is not diminished,
Fully blooming in time.
Eternal open petals of Grace.
Age must indeed come before Beauty
—the artwork of God.

When I was a child, I was drawn to old things, asking questions of my parents and grandparents about various antique objects and their use. I liked collecting the stories they told, and loved hearing about the people who owned the objects. When I was older, I started collecting antiques, giving them stories of my own.

In college, my grandfather sent me a letter, enclosing a check, and telling me, "College kids are always poor so I will send you twenty-five dollars a month to spend on foolish things." I started scouring yard sales, antique stores, and thrift shops in the San Francisco area, scouting out antiques for twenty-five dollars or less. My first purchase was a beautiful but broken antique clock. The next month I used the money to have it repaired, and I still have it today, along with many other of my twenty-five-dollar treasures (an old wooden slatted trunk, a large copper pot, and a glass kerosene lamp, to name a few.)

Over the years, I have received an abundance of antique furniture and objects passed down from relatives; my story merged with their stories, making my own life richer and fuller. I felt I was the guard and caretaker for their memories. The memories brought a more vibrant aesthetic beauty to each piece.

This painting represents the old things I have lived with and loved, and how they became more beautiful with time because of the people they have served. After my dad died, this blue and white plate was discovered in his chest of drawers with my name written on a sticky note on the back. I imagine he intended to give it to me on our next visit, which was on the calendar for the week after his death. The little vase trimmed with silver belonged to my favorite aunt.

Petals from these flowers fell long before I had finished the painting. But I feasted my eyes on their short lives, from their tightly closed beginning to the unfolding of their petals that seemed to reach out to me with words of encouragement. I chose to paint the tulips at the end of their life rather than the beginning—fully opened and about to fall, revealing their hearts—their most exquisite state.

Unfortunately, growing old in our culture is not as easily navigated nor is it as revered as flowers at the end of their lives. Magazines with pictures of models and movie stars, Instagram and social media— where everyone only presents planned faces from the best possible angle—it all produces discontentment when I look in the mirror. Comparing myself with others can be deadly for my confidence. It's a constant fight within me. I would like to stay young and full of life, without wrinkles or saggy skin. But at the same time, because I am beyond middle age, I think of my life as more deeply fulfilled because of the stories I've lived, and my relationships enhanced with beautiful words and memories.

My arthritic hands are becoming crooked, wrinkled, and spotted with age. But as I think back over the years, I'm grateful for all the things my hands have had the opportunity to do. These hands have held other hands and hugged people, written journals, poems, and letters. My hands are not a *thing* of beauty but rather a *tool* to create beauty. These hands have gripped garden tools, guided wheelbarrows, and planted seeds that grew into trees and flowers and fresh produce. They have cleaned houses, refinished furniture, painted rooms, and created art on canvas. These hands have made clothes, created costumes for my kids, and mended socks. These hands have held babies and lifted my children onto swings. These hands have rubbed backs and have given tender caresses. They have prepared thousands of meals, thrown balls, wiped away tears, and washed and folded more clothes than I wish to remember.

It is said, "We wear our heart on our face and the life we lead eventually shows up there." And I do believe it's true, at least for me. My face holds artwork that has taken me years to create, so I'm careful not to mess with it or try to tweak it. I did this recently to one of my paintings and the outcome was disastrous!

Admittedly, I struggle with getting old. I fight it with lotions under my makeup. I try to lecture myself about sun damage and hydrating my skin to keep it young. I sometimes allow my culture to squeeze me into its mold and inform me what is beautiful and what is not. Meanwhile, I give myself pep talks and I moisturize my heart with Scripture that speaks of how women *should* make themselves attractive. "Your beauty should not come from your outward adornments, such as elaborate hairstyles and the wearing of gold jewelry or fine clothes. Instead, it should be that of your inner self, the unfading beauty of a gentle and quiet spirit, which is of great worth in God's sight."[22]

Don't get me wrong; I want to be beautiful, yet intrinsically I know that beauty has to come from within me, and that takes time. Kindness is the best make up I could use. I feel most beautiful when I'm counting all the ways I'm grateful to God, when I think about how I can be kind to someone else: when I give grace to others, overlooking an offense, when I go looking for someone to encourage, and when I write notes of love to my kids or my husband. When love and compassion seep out of me through the windows of my eyes as I gaze at another who is hurting, and when loving words fall generously from my lips, then and only then will true beauty emerge—a face in full bloom, revealing the heart.

"Lord God, please plant Your beauty within my spirit and heart. And help me not to fuss so much about my outward appearance! I need Your 'night cream' that smooths the wrinkles on my heart that are caused by my self-focused attitude, rudeness, and complaining."

"Therefore, we do not lose heart.
Though outwardly we are wasting away, yet inwardly,
we are being renewed day by day."
(2 Corinthians 4:16, NIV)

"Charm is deceptive, and beauty is fleeting,
but a woman who fears the Lord is to be praised.
(Proverbs 31:30, NIV

22. 1 Peter 3:4-5

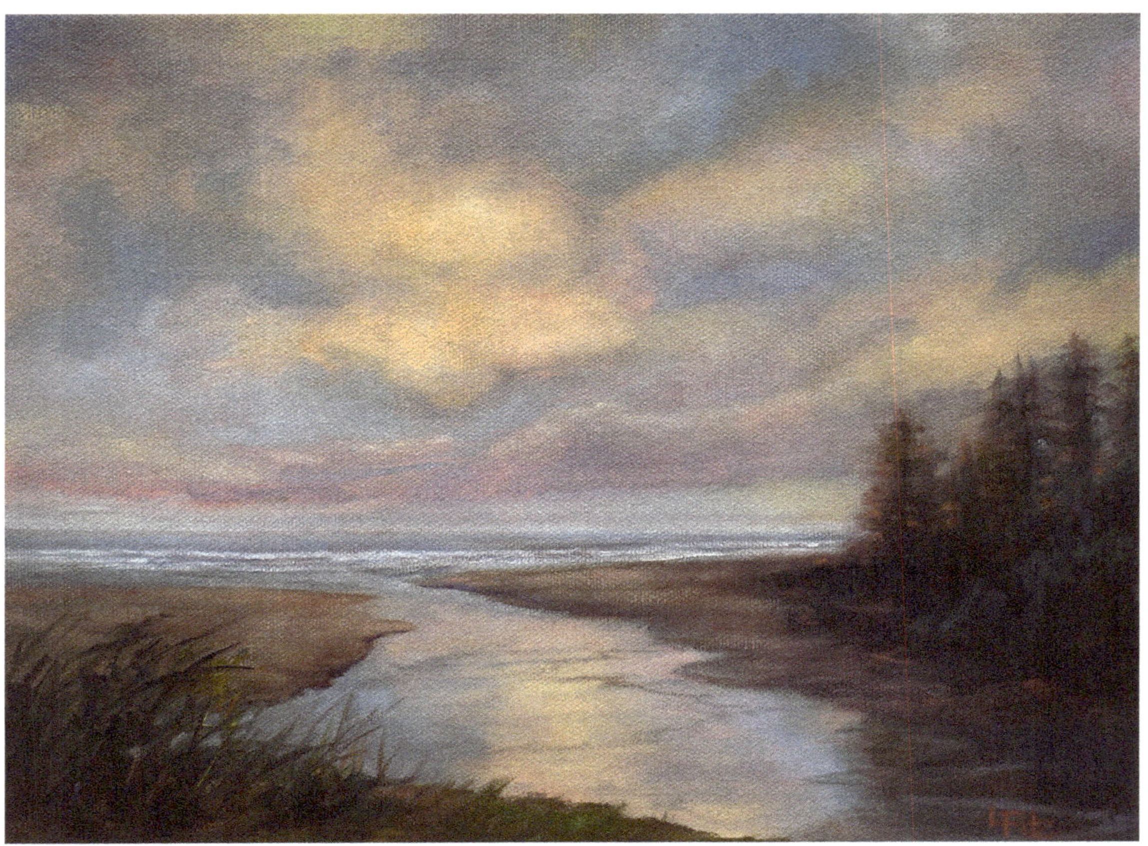

PAINTING, *AFTERGLOW* © 2019 LEIGH D. FITZ (KALALOCH LODGE ON THE WASHINGTON COAST); WRITINGS, 2019

Afterglow

Sunsets draw me into a state of quiet reflection; gratitude closely follows. It's like putting an exclamation mark at the end of the day. Watching the sun go down is amazing but the exquisite part, for me, is the ever-changing colors that light up the clouds and the sky. It's the afterglow show. Nature is clapping, singing its praise to the Creator.

Sunsets settle me, like a baby quieted by its mother's touch. The beauty of the earth and sky at twilight can overwhelm me, bringing me to tears. I feel God's presence more acutely as I breathe deeper and whisper,

"Thank You," to Him, because sometimes I like to imagine that He puts on this show just for me, because He knows me. He knows how much I appreciate a good sunset.

In my youth, when my life was still ahead of me, I rarely gave thought to what I wanted to give to others during my stay here on Earth. I failed to ask myself what I wanted to do to give back. I verged more toward asking myself what I wanted to possess. Truthfully, I wanted to be great at one thing, to be known as someone of worth. I wanted to be loved.

Mistakenly, I thought gathering wealth or being known would bring happiness, but instead I learned quite the opposite was true. Wealth or popularity can be a barrier to friendships. Remembering and cherishing others are paramount, and are essential to being loved yourself. Being loved by God and others is when I've experienced the most profound joy that leaves me filled with gratitude. Contentment lives in those days.

Now, as I'm racing toward the last years of my life, I'm asking what I want to leave behind. I hope that I played a part in other's discovery of God's love for humanity. I pray my words and paintings accompanied someone in this ever-changing and often challenging path of life. I continue to ask God to give me words "to sustain the weary."[23] I'm hoping that I will be remembered as someone who loved God, loved people, and loved to create visual emotions.

At the end of my life, I hope I will be like a sunset as well, reflecting the beauty of God's love. More than anything else, I want my kids and grandkids to know how deeply I loved each one of them. Not everybody gets a chance to say what they want before they die; that's why I want to say it now. I'm hoping that the people I've loved will pause, and be thankful that I existed. Isn't this what we all long for? We want to be remembered, we want be missed, we want to be loved. I want this book to be the "afterglow" or the color and thoughts that linger after sunset. It will remain, full of color after my life has set.

"From the rising of the sun
to the place where it sets,
the name of the Lord is to be praised."
(Psalm 103:3, ESV)

23. Isaiah 50:4

Abundant Thanks

I am eternally grateful for my husband, JD, without whose encouragement this book would never have existed. Thank you, JD, for your love and kind words, your belief in my ability to write this book, and your appreciation for my artwork. You made my goals your own this past year, providing time and space to work, relieving me of housework, errands, and grocery store shopping, just to name a few. Thanks for reading and editing my manuscript more than once and talking over so many changes. You constantly water my soul.

A big thanks to my adult kids—Anne, Kate, and Michael—for your support. You taught me gobs about myself and life. Thank you for your insights and long phone calls. Thank you, Anne, for opening every conversation this past year with the question, "How is your book coming?", for giving me Anne Lamont's very helpful book, *Bird by Bird,* and for continually complimenting my writing (even though we both know you are a better writer than me).

A very special thanks to JoAnn Johnson, for being such a lovingly patient friend and confidante, for diligently lifting my spirits and praying for me, for your reassurances that, in fact, others needed my words—imagine! Thank you for reading and giving me feedback and ideas on my writing and for all the time you took listening as I voiced both my ideas and my doubts. (Also, let's not forget our pinky promise to each other that began this whole process.)

I am indebted to my committed prayer team—my two sisters, Jill Davis and Patti Edwards, who not only diligently prayed for me this last year as I wrote but supported, loved, and have been my cheerleaders my entire life. I am blessed and thankful for Peggy Anderson, Julia Gould, JoAnn Johnson, Jeanie Schneider, Cindy Storrar, and Annette Winters, who agreed to pray for me when this project began. They also did a great job of encouraging, texting, and bolstering me when my doubts came calling, and they constantly said, "I can't wait to have your book in my hands!" I truly hope you all realize the vital role you played in this production!

A big thanks to my editor, Arlyn Lawrence and her team at Inspira Literary Solutions, who not only corrected my mistakes and brought clarity to my writing but who also dished out encouragement in heaps. Thank you, thank you!

I am deeply grateful for my art teacher and friend Madeline Jones, who essentially taught me everything I know about painting, Donna Trent, who taught me plein air painting, and Michael Orwick, for teaching me new techniques and more on plein air, and inspiring me to paint emotion.

Finally, I am so grateful for Tammy Bhang, Linda Hummel, Kim Hunter, and Becky Nelson, whom I've had the privilege of journeying with for over thirty years, through both joy-filled and life-altering challenges. Much of the hard-won wisdom that appears in this book I directly gleaned from these valued women.

About the Author

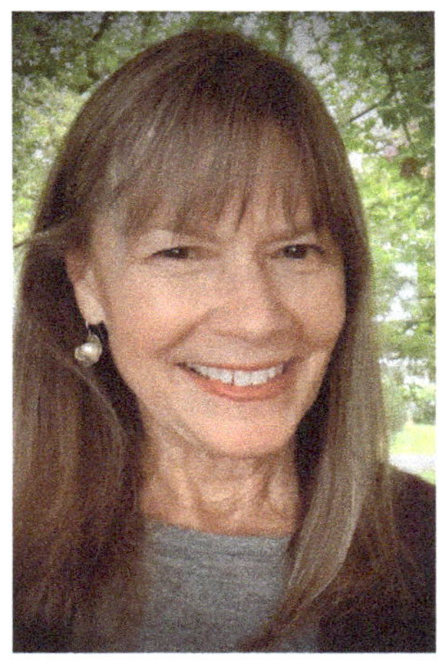

Leigh D. Fitz has journaled and painted for over thirty years. She loves the restoration process—whether it's restoring old homes, gardens, relationships, or her own soul.

Having received her degree in social work, Leigh has always had the desire to assist and serve people who are experiencing difficulty or distressing life issues. She enjoys daily walks, cooking, coffee, and significant conversations with friends.

Leigh and her husband, JD, a retired physician, have two daughters, one son, five grandkids, and a Golden Doodle named Tucker. They make their home in the Pacific Northwest.

www.leighdfitz-artandsoul.com

If you'd like to contact Leigh, her website is

www.leighdfitz-artandsoul.com